LAURA RIDING

GARLAND REFERENCE LIBRARY
OF THE HUMANITIES
(VOL. 224)

the Review

No. 23   5s. 0d.

LAURA RIDING

Essays by
Roy Fuller

Martin
Seymour Smith

A Conversation
with Stephen
Spender

Harold Monro
by Colin Falck

Opinion by
Anthony Thwaite

Photograph of Laura Riding in the 1930's

LAURA RIDING
A Bibliography

Joyce Piell Wexler

GARLAND PUBLISHING, INC. • NEW YORK & LONDON
1981

Library of Congress Cataloging in Publication Data

Wexler, Joyce Piell, 1947–
    Laura Riding, a bibliography.

    (Garland reference library of the humanities ;
v. 224)
    Includes indexes.
    1. Jackson, Laura (Riding), 1901–   —Bibliog-
raphy.   I. Title.
Z8443.4.W48   [PS3519.A363]   016.811′52   80-8481
ISBN 0-8240-9476-X

Printed on acid-free, 250-year-life paper
Manufactured in the United States of America

For Deborah and Sarah,
two young bibliophiles

CONTENTS

ILLUSTRATIONS

ACKNOWLEDGMENTS

Russell Maylone, Director of Special Collections, Northwestern University Library, has offered expert professional advice and warm personal encouragement. His erudition and enthusiasm make him the perfect curator.

I would also like to thank Eric Carpenter, Curator of the Poetry Collection of the State University of New York at Buffalo, and Donald D. Eddy, Curator of the Department of Rare Books of Cornell University, for their valuable assistance. Laura (Riding) Jackson has designated Cornell as the official custodian of her books and papers and has made its collection of her work nearly complete.

PREFACE

Although I have in general adhered to the forms of standard bibliographic practice, Laura Riding's departures from usual publishing practice have made certain deviations desirable. Section A includes all major works by Riding, including books of poetry, essays, stories, letters; pamphlets; translations; collaborations; and periodicals she edited. The ruling principle was to provide a full bibliographic description for any substantial effort.

On the other hand, contributions to books and periodicals are treated briefly. Section B records all contributions of poems to periodicals and books (excluding anthologies). Section C lists all other contributions to periodicals and books. Section D indicates poems reprinted in anthologies. Section E lists entries in reference books because many required Riding's cooperation, and several include autobiographical statements. In these five sections, items are arranged chronologically to demonstrate Riding's development. Section F lists collections of unpublished manuscripts and letters arranged alphabetically by the name of the owner, and Section G, the final grouping of primary works, describes broadcasts and a recording Riding made.

Section H lists articles, books, dissertations, reviews, memoirs, biographical accounts, and criticism—anything that discusses some aspect of Riding's life or work. Items of particular interest are annotated briefly to indicate their character. This register is also organized chronologically.

Because many of Riding's works are scarce, I have described them in more detail than is usual in bibliographies. I have quoted in full the publishing information on all the pages preceding and following the text. Much of this material in the privately printed volumes was probably written by Riding herself, and it conveys the tone of the Seizin Press to some extent. To indicate direct transcription including lineation, I have used the English system of inverted commas and placed my punctuation outside the quotation mark. When I quote dust jacket copy or reviews, I use the standard American form of quotation marks placed after commas and periods.

After the transcription of the title page, each entry includes a description of the collation or format of the book. The size of the sheets, with the vertical dimension first, the system of signatures the printer used, and pagination are described in this section. Signatures and page numbers that are not printed but can be inferred are in brackets. When a book is unsigned, gatherings are not inferred. After the summary of pages, a transcription of each page before and after the text appears. Most publishing and printing information is presented this way and is not re-peated elsewhere.

The description of binding follows. It proceeds from front to back to spine. If no design is mentioned, it should be assumed none appears. Edges of sheets are described as trimmed, un-trimmed, colored, as necessary. If I have seen a dust jacket, I describe it in a separate paragraph.

Paper is termed "laid" if it has a chain and line design, "wove" if it does not. Hand-made and watermarked papers are noted when they appear. Endpapers are described in the same way in this section.

The contents of each book are listed as they appear. The notes at the end of each entry indicate the publication date and price listed in the *English Catalogue of Books* or the American *Cumulative Book Index*. Any other points of interest are mentioned here. In addition to examining the books myself, I have incorporated information provided by Nancy Cunard's history of the Hours Press, Hugh Ford's account of the Seizin Press, and Fred Higginson's bibliography of the works of Robert Graves. An asterisk preceding an item indicates that I have relied on photocopies, and two asterisks precede items I have not seen.

INTRODUCTION

"Laura Riding" may be the outstanding achievement of the woman born Laura Reichenthal in New York City, January 16, 1901. She was the middle child of a father who considered himself a non-religious Jewish Socialist and a mother who fancied herself an invalid. As a scholarship student she attended Cornell University, where she met Louis Gottschalk, a young history instructor. They were married in 1920, and she changed her name to "Laura Riding Gottschalk" because, she said, "Laura Reichenthal Gottschalk" would be unwieldy. Nevertheless, she insisted her husband take her name; even after their divorce he continued to call himself "Louis Reichenthal Gottschalk" because of his great respect for her father. She left Cornell before graduation and accompanied her husband on the academic circuit from Urbana, Illinois, to Louisville, Kentucky. He expected her to be a "more-intelligent-than-most" faculty wife, but never anticipated the fervor for a poetic vocation she demonstrated after their marriage.

Riding began to submit her poems to little magazines in the early 1920's and found her work welcomed. Harriet Monroe published a few of her poems in *Poetry* and eagerly offered advice to advance her career. The Fugitive Group in Nashville, which included John Crowe Ransom, Allen Tate, Robert Penn Warren, and Donald Davidson, awarded her prizes and invited her to become a member. Her letters to Davidson at this time express her personal loneliness and sense of isolation as a poet. The Fugitives were the first to offer her professional comradeship.

In 1925 Riding moved to New York City in search of a literary community. She and her husband were divorced, both said, because he was unable to sympathize with her devotion to poetry. She continued to use her married name, however. Working for a publisher, doing some translation and reviewing, she "starved" in the bohemian tradition of poets. She became a friend of Hart Crane and observed what she later called the predatory effect of the literary jungle on his work. Drawn to the metropolis by a desire for colleagues, she was soon repelled by the competitiveness she found there.

In 1926 she accepted an invitation from Robert Graves and his wife, Nancy Nicholson, to collaborate on a book about modernist poetry. Riding arrived in London soon after Christmas. A sign of the changes in her life is the dedication of her first volume of poems, *The Close Chaplet*, to her sister and to Nancy Nicholson. The title was inspired by Graves's poem "The Nape of the Neck," from which the book's epigraph is taken. She dedicated her next book, *Voltaire*, to "L.G.," yet had her married name cancelled after the title page was printed (see illustration, p. 8). Only with the publication of *A Survey of Modernist Poetry* in 1927 did she assume the authorial name "Laura Riding."

Under this signature, she published some of the best poetry of the 1920's and 1930's. Writing with insight, precision, and wit, she articulated her sense of being a woman with a mind. Her consciousness of the difficulties this caused pervades her work. She believed speech was the natural complement of thought; the possibility of inarticulate thought never existed for her. Her experience with words that were untrue made her loathe anything less than what she called the fidelity of word to thought, or truth. Poetry became the supreme value in her life because it offered a stable way to unite speech and thought.

The title of Riding's 1928 volume of poems, *Love as Love, Death as Death*, expressed the principle underlying her work. She wanted to know love as love, death as death, each thing as itself, not what it was like. As a result, her poems avoided metaphor in favor of presenting parallel cases that illuminated each other while remaining distinct. Her poems were as literal as she could make them. The figurative use of words seemed to her too close to lying.

Love as Love was the first publication of the Seizin Press, which Riding and Graves founded. Its goals included the desire to publish the kind of writing its owners had advocated in their criticism. The home of the press in St. Peter's Square, Hammersmith, sheltered a literary cottage industry. By 1929 it had issued poems by Riding and Graves and *An Acquaintance with Description* by Gertrude Stein.

Its schedule was interrupted when Riding stepped out a second-story window on Easter Sunday, 1929. Speculation about the reasons for her suicide attempt instantly became a subject of literary gossip. Her gradual physical recovery produced extraordinary psychological results. She began to think of herself as having suffered a physical "death" that freed a purely spiritual "self." She spoke of herself as "unreal," a word she had used earlier to mean honed to an essence. Everything transitory, accidental, and personal fell away. Only mind remained.

An indirect result of Riding's "leap," as she began to call it, was that Graves and his wife were divorced. He and Riding left London as soon as she was able to travel, and they decided to settle in Deyá, a small village in Majorca. They had their hand press moved there and resumed their literary production. Among their more ambitious projects of the 1930's was *Epilogue*, a periodical with the format of a book. Edited by Riding, the review was designed to state "final" truth about a wide range of subjects. *Epilogue*, the Seizin Press, and the presence of Riding and Graves attracted writers who wanted to work in Deyá. Until the Spanish Civil War forced them to leave in the summer of 1936, Majorca was an enclave for Riding's circle.

After travelling in Europe, Riding and Graves came to New Hope, Pennsylvania, with a group of friends from Majorca in search of a new literary home. In 1938 Riding and Graves published impressive volumes of *Collected Poems*, and Graves's dedication pays tribute to Riding's contributions to his work. But in 1939 the working relationship that had been so fruitful for both of them ended for personal and professional reasons. Her hopes for Graves, in particular, and poetry, in general, were exhausted. She renounced poetry in favor of linguistic study as a more accessible path to truth-telling. This phase of her life was marked by another name change: in 1941 she married Schuyler B. Jackson and began to call herself "Laura (Riding) Jackson."

As Mrs. Jackson, she published no book until 1970. The abrupt silence after fluent speech constituted a withdrawal from literature for moral and, I believe, psychological motives. She turned from the uniqueness of poetic expression to the utility of lexicography. Isolated in Wabasso, Florida, she and her husband decided to produce a new kind of dictionary. Devoting themselves to their chosen task with the strictness of monks, they sought the intrinsic principles of language that would enable them to give each word an absolute definition. The deficiency of other dictionaries, they felt, was the use of synonyms to suggest what a word meant. This work was to be called "Rational Meaning: A New Foundation for the Definition of Words"; only explanatory essays have appeared thus far.

In 1970 Mrs. Jackson permitted her *Selected Poems: In Five Sets* to appear with a statement of the reasons she renounced poetry. In 1972 she presented *The Telling* in book form, the culmination of her lifelong effort to make language yield truth. Choosing her words for their meanings and disregarding style, she tried to articulate ultimate realities of the universe. Liberated from the restraints of form, she felt confident she could reveal the spiritual essence of human nature, known to her because she was the first to discover the link between language and spiritual knowledge.

Regarding her career as a constant progression toward truth, Mrs. Jackson considers *The Telling* superior. Since its publication, she has rebuked critics who have attempted to praise her poetry without accepting her prophetic writings. A series of letters to editors indicates the extent of her continuing effort to control interpretations and evaluations of her work. Until a few years ago, she tried to suppress *14A*, written with George Ellidge in 1934, and *Convalescent Conversations*, signed with the pseudonym "Madeleine Vara" in 1936. She still refuses to acknowledge *No Decency Left*, attributed to "Barbara Rich," the name of the heroine, which appeared in 1932, though Robert Graves identified himself and Riding as the authors.

I suspect that Riding also wrote much of *A Mistake Somewhere*, published anonymously as a Seizin-Constable book in 1935. It was advertised on the dust jacket of her *Progress of Stories* that year:

> Two young free-lance journalists, not long married, and an elder fascinating woman with whom the husband has fallen in love, try to be honest with one another. They decide to

put down separate accounts of their story, as the basis for an understanding. The three documents are printed side by side.

Although the story is told from three points of view, the reader's interest concentrates on the tensions in the husband, Richard, as he vacillates between two steady poles. Christine, a rich divorcee ten years older than he, offers exciting worldliness, and Helen, his wife, provides loyal stability. Struggling to be virtuous, Richard wishes he could love Helen with the passion he feels for Christine. The two women sympathize with each other and with Richard, but when Helen discovers that her patient tolerance of his inability to choose one of them makes her miserable, she concludes that she has made "a mistake somewhere."

Each character's account begins with detailed memories of childhood and adolescent experiences. The particularity is unlike Riding's poetry but similar to her other suppressed books and the more realistic sections of *Progress of Stories*. While neither Christine nor Helen equals Riding, both resemble her in some ways. Riding had been involved in romantic triangles, and she understood the shifting conflicts and alliances they could generate. Certain passages, like this one from Helen's account, have a characteristic Riding ring:

> My writing was an act of conscience, but Richard's was a frolic. He could do almost anything with a pen. He wrote humourously, plaintively, excitingly—but his themes were often borrowed and his style too variable to be called a style of his own. I had my own themes but no style at all. The success of my work depended entirely on whether I could repeat on paper what I thought to myself: there was no question of "literary" charm with me. (p. 283)

Helen's disparagement of Richard's popularity, her contempt for style separated from theme, and her goal of articulating her thoughts echo Riding's values.

In addition to textual evidence, Riding's attempt to suppress the book suggests she was responsible for it. She has even prohibited the Poetry Collection of the State University of New York at Buffalo from permitting anyone to see its copy. Although she allowed Hugh Ford to list the book in his article on the Seizin

Press which she approved, he was unable to describe either this book or *Convalescent Conversations*. Ford's article documents the extraordinary editorial control Riding maintained over all Seizin publications.

T.S. Matthews' account of his association with Riding in the 1930's in *Jacks or Better* also attests to her ubiquitous presence in Seizin books; Matthews felt his own Seizin-Constable book, *The Moon's No Fool* (1936), should have been signed by her. Riding's revisions, suppressions, and censorship consistently focus on the most autobiographical parts of her work, and *A Mistake Some-where* fits this pattern. Apparently she considered the story so recognizable that it had to be issued anonymously.

For other writing that she did not want to be associated with her poetry, Riding invented pseudonyms. The most frequent was the euphonious "Madeleine Vara." She signed *Convalescent Conversations* with this name probably to prevent readers from connecting it with her convalescence in 1929 following her widely publicized suicide attempt. She used the same name in *Epilogue* for a different reason: she wanted to conceal the extent of her own participation in each issue.

"Lilith Outcome" was a less serious attempt to masquerade. Clearly a symbolic name, this signature was used when Riding knew she would be detected but wanted to assume a persona. "Lilith Outcome" was cited as the author of *Automancy*, a nonexistent book that provided the epigraph for *Experts Are Puzzled* (1930), and of Riding's own letters in *Everybody's Letters* (1933).

I discovered another pseudonym among the papers of J.B. Pinker and Sons, Literary Agents, at Northwestern University. A letter from one of Pinker's readers, M.F. Allen, dated August 13, 1927, reported on a manuscript captioned, "Flickwerk by Lilian Reiter." Someone in Pinker's office added in pencil, "= Laura Riding." The reader's opinion was favorable:

> I don't think this book would go in England, but as the author says it might be quite successful in the States, where they seem very interested in Jewish stories. Personally I found the part dealing with the boy's life in Galicia more interesting than the part where he lives in New York. The writer evidently has an intimate knowledge of Jewish life as it was lived in the eighties in Galicia and Russia, and also with the characteristics of the Jew. I wonder if she is one

herself, I should think so. I found her much more interest-
ing than Miss Hannah Berman, much simpler and more
direct.

Nevertheless, the book did not find a publisher.[1] Even its author
did not want to claim it. "Laura Riding" was reserved for the
writing she deemed befitting a serious poet.

Although Riding obstructs critical and biographical accounts,
she is a reliable source for information about the history of her
publications. The checklist Alan Clark compiled with her help
for *It Has Taken Long* (1976) mentions a 46-page pamphlet that I
have been unable to locate. It is *Len Lye and the Problem of Popular
Films*, signed "L.R." and published by the Seizin Press in London
in 1938. Hugh Ford also reports that she described this pamphlet to him.

Neither Clark nor Ford lists any copies of the Subjects of
Knowledge series advertised in a 1936 Seizin-Constable bro-
chure I saw at the Poetry Collection in Buffalo:

> A series of simply written books, for schoolroom or general
> reading, in which the subjects are treated both historically
> and critically by a committee of Seizin authors.

A pamphlet on "Schools" was to be a "summary of the history of
schools and educational ideas throughout the world." Another
on "Poets" would tell how "there came to be professional poets,
the development of various types of poems, the attitude to poets
and poetry during different periods of history." Since Riding
cooperated with both Clark and Ford, I assume the series never
appeared. The impulse behind it was realized in *Epilogue*.

The "Laura Riding" years, 1927–1938, are the foundation of a
secure literary reputation. The prodigious amount of writing
she did is overshadowed only by its quality. Her stories, essays,
novels, and publishing ventures represent her effort to reach a
wider audience than her poems attracted. But it was the poetry
she cared most about. It received her serious effort and established her importance. She made it portray a woman wrestling
with words to know herself, and winning at last.

---

1. Riding asked Pinker to return the manuscript to her (postcard dated 18
   November 1927, Berg Collection, New York Public Library).

LAURA RIDING

A. MAJOR WORKS:
BOOKS AND PERIODICALS,
INCLUDING COLLABORATIONS AND TRANSLATIONS

A1   THE CLOSE CHAPLET   1926

a. First British edition

THE CLOSE CHAPLET | BY | LAURA RIDING GOTTSCHALK | [publisher's
device] | Published by | Leonard & Virginia Woolf at The Hogarth
Press | 52 Tavistock Square, London, W.C. 1 | 1926

Collation: 7 1/8 x 4 7/8 in., [1]^8 2-5^8, pp. [1-6] 7-76 [77-
80]. [1]: 'THE CLOSE CHAPLET'. [2]: blank. [3]: title page.
[4]: '[9 lines of verse] | ROBERT GRAVES. | Printed in Great
Britain by | NEILL & CO., LTD., EDINBURGH.' [5]: 'TO | MY
SISTER ISABEL | AND TO | NANCY NICHOLSON'. [6]: blank. 7-8:
Contents. 9-[77]: text. [77]: colophon. [78-80]: blank.

Binding: Blue-gray paper over boards. Buff label (1 7/8 x
3 1/4 in.) on front printed in black. A double rule border
encloses: '*THE* | *CLOSE CHAPLET* | *LAURA GOTTSCHALK*'. Back
blank. All edges trimmed.

Paper: Cream wove paper, including endpapers.

Contents:
 9 As Well As Any Other
10 The Quids
12 Mortal
13 The Sad Boy
15 The Nightmare
16 Lucrece and Nara
18 Ahead and Around
20 One
21 Body's Head
29 Body in the Clouds

THE CLOSE CHAPLET

BY

LAURA RIDING GOTTSCHALK

Published by
Leonard & Virginia Woolf at The Hogarth Press
52 Tavistock Square, London, W.C. 1
1926

Title page of *The Close Chaplet* (A1)

Note: Published in October, 1926, at 5s.

b. First American edition

THE CLOSE CHAPLET | BY | LAURA RIDING GOTTSCHALK | ADELPHI
COMPANY | *Publishers* | NEW YORK

Collation: Identical to British edition.

Binding: Identical to British edition.

Paper: Identical to British edition.

Notes: Priced at $1.75. Although this is Riding's first
volume of poems, a ghost called "Poems," attributed to Greenberg Publishing Company, 64 pages, $1.75, appears in the *Cumu-
lative Book Index* for 1926 and in the *U.S. Catalogue of Books
in Print* for 1928. This title also appears in *Publishers'
Weekly*, March 13, 1926, but the publisher is listed as Adelphi.

The discrepancy is due to Greenberg's acquisition of the Adelphi Company effective October 1, 1926. Greenberg continued to
use the Adelphi imprint, which also appears in *Anatole France
at Home* (A2), until January 1, 1928. Apparently Riding's
first book of poems received its present title after it was
first announced. Nevertheless, an advertisement in *Contemporaries and Snobs* (A5) in 1928 announced that *First Poems* was
to be published by Jonathan Cape and Doran. The dust jacket
of *Poems: A Joking Word* (A9) in 1930 also cited this ghost
volume as a source in addition to *The Close Chaplet*: "It includes the substance not only of *The Close Chaplet* published
in 1926 and of *Love as Love, Death as Death*, published in 1928,
but also the deferred *First Poems* announced some seasons ago;
and certain later poems."

A2   ANATOLE FRANCE AT HOME   1926

ANATOLE FRANCE | AT HOME | *By* | MARCEL LeGOFF | *Translated by* |
LAURA RIDING GOTTCHALK | *With unpublished photographs and
documents* | ADELPHI COMPANY | *Publishers 1926*

Collation: 9 x 6 in., unsigned, pp. [i-ii] iii-v [vi] vii [viii]
ix-x [xi-xii] 1-197 [198-200]. 4 plates on coated stock before
p. [i] [verso], after p. 52 [recto], after p. 116 [recto], and
after p. 180 [recto]. Extra leaf front and back. [i]: title
page. [ii]: 'COPYRIGHT, 1926, BY ADELPHI COMPANY | THE VAIL-
BALLOU PRESS | BINGHAMTON AND NEW YORK'. iii-v: Contents.
[vi]: blank. vii: 'ILLUSTRATIONS'. [viii]: blank. ix-x:
Foreword. [xi]: 'ANATOLE FRANCE | AT HOME'. [xii]: blank.
1-197: text. [198-200]: blank.

Binding and dust jacket: Black cloth over boards. Front printed
in gold. A decorative rectangle encloses: '*ANATOLE FRANCE* |
AT HOME | [rule broken by fleur-de-lis] | *MARCEL LE GOFF*'.
Spine printed in gold: '*ANATOLE* | *FRANCE* | *AT HOME* | [rule] |
LE GOFF | ADELPHI'. Back blank. All edges trimmed.
  Buff dust jacket printed in red and black. Front reprints
photograph that is used as frontispiece.

Paper: Cream wove paper, including endpapers.

Contents:
  1   The First Conversations
  6   Anatole France and the War
 24   The War and Literature

Illustrations:

Notes: In the *Cumulative Book Index*, the listed publisher is Greenberg, which operated the Adelphi Company from October 1, 1926, to January 1, 1928. The price was $2.50. Riding's name was misspelled on the title page.

A3   VOLTAIRE   1927

VOLTAIRE | A Biographical Fantasy | LAURA RIDING GOTTSCHALK [last name cancelled by double rule] | Printed & published by L. & V. Woolf | at The Hogarth Press, 52 Tavistock Square | 1927

Collation: 8 x 5 1/2 in., unsigned, pp. [i-ii] [1-4] 5-30. [i]: blank. [ii] frontispiece--an engraving captioned 'VOLTAIRE.' [1]: title page. [2]: 'To | L.G.'. [3]: 'Fore word', dated 1921. [4]: 'Au bord de l'infini ton coeur doit s'arrêter; | Là commence un abyme, il faut le respecter. | VOLTAIRE'. 5-27: text. 28-30: 'THE ARGUMENT'.

Binding: Heavy black paper folded to form 2 1/2 in. front and back flaps. Buff label (1 7/8 x 3 3/8 in.) on front with double rule border enclosing 'VOLTAIRE | LAURA RIDING'. Back blank. Only top edge trimmed.

Paper: Cream laid paper, including endpapers.

VOLTAIRE

A Biographical Fantasy

LAURA RIDING ~~GOTTSCHALK~~

Printed & published by L. & V. Woolf
at The Hogarth Press, 52 Tavistock Square
1927

VOLTAIRE.

Frontispiece and title page of *Voltaire* (A3); "GOTTSCHALK" cancelled by hand

Notes: Although published in November, 1927, at 3s. 6d., the
Foreword is dated 1921. The dedication to "L.G." links the
book to Louis Gottschalk, though Riding had her married surname
cancelled after the title page was printed. "The Argument"
following the text is a summary of the "plot" keyed to line
numbers.

Reprints were issued by Folcroft Press (Folcroft, Pa.) in
1969 and 1977 and by Norwood Editions (Norwood, Pa.) in 1977
and 1978.

A4   A SURVEY OF MODERNIST POETRY   1927

a. First British edition

A SURVEY OF | MODERNIST POETRY | BY | LAURA RIDING AND ROBERT
GRAVES | [publisher's device] | LONDON | WILLIAM HEINEMANN
LTD. | 1927

Collation: 7 1/2 x 5 in., [A]^8 B-S^8 T^4, pp. [1-8] 9-291 [292]
293-295 [296]. [1]: 'A SURVEY OF | MODERNIST POETRY'. [2]:
blank. [3]: title page. [4] '*Printed in Great Britain by*
R. & R. CLARK, LIMITED, *Edinburgh*'. [5]: 'NOTE | This book
represents a word-by-word collabora- | tion; except for the
last chapter, which is a | revision by both authors for the
purposes of this | volume of an essay separately written and
printed | by one of them'. [6]: blank. [7]: Contents. [8]:
blank. 9-291: text. [292]: blank. 293-295: 'INDEX OF |
PRINCIPAL PROPER NAMES'. [296]: blank.

Binding and dust jacket: Buff paper over boards printed with red
pattern. Black cloth on spine extends 1/4 in. onto front and
back. Spine printed in gold: 'A SURVEY | OF MODERNIST |
POETRY | LAURA RIDING | AND | ROBERT GRAVES | HEINEMANN'.
Top and fore-edges trimmed.

Dust jacket is buff with red printing. Front displays title
and authors' names between decorative brackets. Back advertises *Poems: 1914-1926* by Robert Graves. Copy on inside flap
reads: "This is a sympathetic and authoritative study of the
untraditional elements in modern poetry--the first of its kind.
The authors treat of the work of T.S. Eliot, Edith, Osbert and
Sacheverell Sitwell, E.E. Cummings, Gertrude Stein, Marianne
Moore, John Crowe Ransom and of other 'modernist' rather than
merely 'modern' poets of England and America; showing what
standards these set themselves, and to what extent they justify

their theories." Back flap advertises *The Land* by V. Sackville-West and *Willie Lamberton* by Elizabeth Manning.

Paper: Cream laid paper, including endpapers.

Contents:

Notes: 1000 copies at 7s. 6d. were published November 3, 1927. The method of textual analysis demonstrated in the third chapter is the focus of a dispute about the origin of the New Criticism. Riding's position appears in "Correspondence," *Modern Language Quarterly*, 32 (December, 1971), 447-448 (C44).

Reprints were issued by Haskell House (New York) in 1969; Folcroft Library Editions (Folcroft, Pa.) in 1971; Norwood Editions (Norwood, Pa.) in 1976, 1977, and 1978; and R. West (Philadelphia) in 1977.

**al. *Second British impression (1929)*

A SURVEY OF | MODERNIST POETRY | BY | LAURA RIDING AND ROBERT GRAVES | [publisher's device] | LONDON | WILLIAM HEINEMANN LTD. | 1929

Collation: Identical to first British edition except p. [4] has impression and printer's notices.

Binding: Black cloth over boards. Front and back blank. Spine printed in gold: 'A SURVEY | OF MODERNIST POETRY | LAURA RIDING | AND | ROBERT GRAVES | HEINEMANN'. Top and fore-edges trimmed.

Paper: Cream laid paper, including endpapers.

Notes: Published in September, 1929, at 7s. 6d. This impression is cited in Higginson's bibliography (H111), but I have not seen it.

b. First American edition (1928)

A SURVEY OF | MODERNIST POETRY | BY | LAURA RIDING AND ROBERT GRAVES | *Garden City, New York* | DOUBLEDAY, DORAN & COMPANY, INC. | 1928

Collation: Identical to British edition.

Binding: Gray paper over boards. Front and back blank. Red cloth on spine extends 1 in. onto front and back. 2 in. gray label on spine printed in red: '[decorative rule] | A SURVEY | OF MODERNIST | POETRY | [decorative rule] | LAURA RIDING | *and* | ROBERT GRAVES | [decorative rule]'. Only top edge trimmed.

Paper: Cream laid paper, including endpapers.

Notes: Only the title page and binding differ from British edition since both were printed in Britain. American publication of 500 copies at $2.00 each appeared a year later than the British edition. A reprint of this edition was issued by Scholarly Press (St. Clair Shores, Mich.) in 1972.

A5   CONTEMPORARIES AND SNOBS   1928

a. First British edition

CONTEMPORARIES | AND SNOBS | By | LAURA RIDING | [publisher's device] | JONATHAN CAPE | THIRTY BEDFORD SQUARE LONDON

Collation: 7 1/2 x 5 in., [A]^8 B–Q^8, pp. [1–4] 5 [6–8] 9–121 [122] 123–199 [200] 201–255 [256]. [1]: 'CONTEMPORARIES AND SNOBS'. [2]: blank. [3]: title page. [4]: 'FIRST PUBLISHED IN MCMXXVIII | MADE & PRINTED IN GREAT BRITAIN | BY BUTLER & TANNER LTD | FROME AND | LONDON | [ornament]'. 5: Contents. [6]: blank. [7]: 'CONTEMPORARIES | AND SNOBS'. [8]: blank. 9–121: text. [122]: 'NOTE' [explaining relationship between

Parts I and II]. 123-199: text. [200]: blank. 201-255: text.
[256]: 'BY THE SAME AUTHOR | POETRY | *The Close Chaplet*, Hogarth
Press, 1926. | *Voltaire*, Hogarth Press, 1927. | *First Poems*,
Jonathan Cape and the George H. | Doran Co. [forthcoming]. |
Love As Love, Death As Death, Seizin Press [forth- | coming]. |
PROSE | *Survey of Modernist Poetry* (Laura Riding and | Robert
Graves), Heinemann and the George | H. Doran Co., 1927. |
Anthologies Against Poetry (Laura Riding and | Robert Graves),
Jonathan Cape and the | George H. Doran Co. [forthcoming].'

Binding: Beige cloth over boards. Front blank. Back blind-
stamped with publisher's device. Spine printed in blue:
'CONTEM- | PORARIES | AND | SNOBS | [ornament] | LAURA |
RIDING | JONATHAN CAPE'. Top edge colored gray. All edges
trimmed.

Paper: Cream wove paper, including endpapers.

Contents:
9	1. Poetry & the Literary Universe
9	I. Shame of the Person
18	II. Poetry, Out of Employment, Writes on Unemployment
31	III. Escapes from the Zeitgeist
56	IV. Poetic Reality and Critical Unreality
79	V. Poetry and Progress
97	VI. The Higher Snobbism
123	2. T.E. Hulme, the New Barbarism, & Gertrude Stein
201	3. The Facts in the Case of Monsieur Poe

Notes: Published at 7s. 6d. in February, 1928. Although the
list of books "By the Same Author" on p. [256] includes *First
Poems*, this volume never materialized. A partial explanation
appears on the dust jacket blurb of *Poems: A Joking Word*,
which states that this collection includes the contents of the
projected volume. The ghost volume was also announced as *Poems*,
to be published by Greenberg Publishing Co. in 1926 at $1.75,
but it was superseded by *The Close Chaplet*. *Anthologies Against
Poetry* is also listed prematurely on p. [256]; it became *A
Pamphlet Against Anthologies* five months later.

b. First American edition

CONTEMPORARIES | AND SNOBS | By | LAURA RIDING | GARDEN CITY |
NEW YORK | DOUBLEDAY DORAN & COMPANY, INC. | 1928

Collation: Identical to British edition except p. [4] omits
the date of first publication.

Binding: Gray paper over boards. Front and back blank. Maroon cloth on spine extends 1 in. onto front and back. Gray paper label (2 1/8 x 1 1/8 in.) on spine printed in red: '[decorative rule] | CONTEMPORARIES | AND SNOBS | [decorative rule] | LAURA | RIDING | [decorative rule]'. All edges trimmed.

Paper: Cream wove paper, including endpapers.

Notes: Published at $2.00. Both editions were printed in Great Britain.
   A reprint was issued by Scholarly Press (St. Clair Shores, Mich.) in 1971.

A6   ANARCHISM IS NOT ENOUGH   1928

a. First British edition

[swash letters] *ANARCHISM* is not enough | [swung dash] | Laura Riding | JONATHAN CAPE | London

Collation: 7 7/8 x 5 3/8 in., [A]^8 B-0^8, pp. [1-4] 5 [6-8] 9-224. [1]: 'ANARCHISM IS NOT ENOUGH | [publisher's device]'. [2]: blank. [3]: title page. [4]: 'FIRST PUBLISHED MCMXXVIII | PRINTED IN GREAT BRITAIN BY | BUTLER & TANNER LTD | FROME'. 5: Contents. [6]: blank. [7]: 'ANARCHISM IS NOT ENOUGH'. [8]: blank. 9-224: text.

Binding: Blue cloth over boards. Front blank. Back blind-stamped with publisher's device. Spine printed in gold: 'ANARCHISM | IS NOT | ENOUGH | [ornament] | LAURA | RIDING | JONATHAN CAPE'. Top and fore-edges trimmed.

Paper: Cream wove paper, including endpapers.

Contents:

Note: Published in May, 1928, at 7s. 6d.

b. First American edition

[swash letters] *ANARCHISM* | is not enough | [swung dash] |
Laura Riding | GARDEN CITY | NEW YORK | DOUBLEDAY, DORAN &
COMPANY, INC. | 1928

Collation: 7 3/4 x 5 3/8 in.   Identical to British edition except for publisher's name on title page and omission of the
date of first publication on p. [4].

Binding: Orange paper over boards.   Front and back blank.
Black cloth on spine extends 1 in. onto front and back.   Orange
label (2 1/8 x 1 in.) on spine printed in black: '[thick
rule] | anarchism | is | not | enough | [thick rule] | laura |
riding | [thick rule]'.   All edges trimmed.

Paper: Identical to British edition.

Contents: Identical to British edition.

Note: Priced at $2.50.

A7   A PAMPHLET AGAINST ANTHOLOGIES   1928

a. First British edition

A Pamphlet | AGAINST ANTHOLOGIES | by | LAURA RIDING | AND ROBERT

GRAVES | [publisher's device] | JONATHAN CAPE | THIRTY BEDFORD
SQUARE | LONDON

Collation: 7 1/2 x 5 in., [A]^8 B-M^8, pp. [1-4] 5 [6] 7-8 [9-10]
11-192. [1]: 'A PAMPHLET AGAINST ANTHOLOGIES'. [2]: blank.
[3]: title page. [4]: 'FIRST PUBLISHED MCMXXVIII | PRINTED IN
GREAT BRITAIN BY | BUTLER & TANNER LTD | FROME'. 5: Contents.
[6]: blank. 7-8: Foreword. [9]: 'A PAMPHLET AGAINST
ANTHOLOGIES'. [10]: blank. 11-192: text.

Binding and dust jacket: Orange cloth over boards. Front blank.
Back blind-stamped with publisher's device. Spine printed in
gold: 'PAMPHLET | AGAINST | ANTHOLOGIES | [ornament] | RIDING |
& GRAVES | JONATHAN CAPE'. Top and fore-edges trimmed.
   Buff dust jacket displays title, authors' and publisher's
names printed in black inside a red decorative rectangle.
Publisher's device also in red. Back advertises *Contemporaries
and Snobs* and quotes favorable reviews it received from Arnold
Bennett in *The Evening Standard*, the *Times Literary Supplement*,
The Observer, and *The Yorkshire Post*.

Paper: Cream wove paper, including endpapers.

Contents:

Notes: Published in July, 1928, at 7s. 6d., this book was
provisionally titled "Anthologies Against Poetry" and announced
at the end of *Contemporaries and Snobs*. Dust jacket description reads, in part: "A distinction is drawn between the
legitimate anthology (of rare occurrence), which is a port-
folio of fugitive verses, and the ever multiplying 'popular
anthology,' a display of stock poetical 'beauties' and conceits
by critical bagmen for a simple-minded public. An analysis is
made of numerous anthologies, ancient and modern, and of
favourite anthology lyrics. Since so much modern poetry is
written in the shadow of the popular anthology, this book covers
a wider ground than its title at first suggests."
   The Foreword emphasizes that this book, like *A Survey of*

Modernist Poetry, is a word-by-word collaboration and rebukes seven reviewers who ignored this note in the earlier book.

b. First American edition

A Pamphlet | AGAINST ANTHOLOGIES | by | LAURA RIDING | AND ROBERT GRAVES | GARDEN CITY, NEW YORK | DOUBLEDAY, DORAN & COMPANY, INC. | 1928

Collation: Identical to British edition except p. [4] omits the date of first publication.

Binding: Buff paper over boards. Front and back blank. Maroon cloth on spine extends 1 in. onto front and back. 2 3/8 in. buff paper label on spine printed in red: '[decorative rule] | A | PAMPHLET | AGAINST | ANTHOLOGIES | [decorative rule] | RIDING | *and* | GRAVES | [decorative rule]'. All edges trimmed.

Paper: Cream wove paper, including endpapers.

Notes: Published at $2.00 and printed in Great Britain. A reprint was issued by the AMS Press (New York) in 1970.

A8   LOVE AS LOVE, DEATH AS DEATH   1928

LOVE AS LOVE, | DEATH AS DEATH | BY | LAURA RIDING | [publisher's device] | Printed and published at The Seizin Press | Hammersmith London 1928

Collation: 8 x 5 1/2 in., unsigned, pp. [i-viii] 1-64. [i]: 'LOVE AS LOVE, DEATH AS DEATH'. [ii]: 'SEIZIN ONE | 175 numbered copies of this edition have been | printed, and this is no. [written] 47 | [signed] Laura Riding | SEIZIN TWO: AN ACQUAINTANCE WITH DESCRIPTION | BY GERTRUDE STEIN. | SEIZIN THREE: POEMS 1929 BY ROBERT GRAVES. | SEIZIN FOUR: NO TROUBLE BY LEN LYE. | (to follow)'. [iii]: title page. [iv]: blank. [v-vi]: Contents. [vii-viii]: blank. 1-64: text.

Binding: Beige cloth over boards. Front and back blank. Spine printed in gold lengthwise: 'LOVE AS LOVE, DEATH AS DEATH'. All edges trimmed.

Paper: Cream laid paper watermarked with a hammer and anvil, a

monogram superimposing B and S, and a crest including the words
'BRITISH HAND MADE'. Same endpapers.

Contents:

1   The Map of Places
2   Death as Death
3   How Blind and Bright
5   Footfalling
6   Though in One Time
7   Ding-Donging
8   If This Reminds
9   The Tiger
16 The Rugged Black of Anger
18 The Number
19 All Nothing, Nothing
22 The Troubles of a Book
24 And This Is Loveliness
25 That Ancient Line
27 Fine Fellow Son of a Poor Fellow
29 Address from Pride in Person
31 Dear Growth
33 Originally
35 Loss of Reason
36 World's End
37 Sea, False Philosophy
39 Helen's Faces
40 Sea Ghost
41 O Vocables of Love
42 Happy Possessor and Industrious Spirit
44 Ode to the Triumph of Bodily Intelligence
46 Sleep Contravened
48 By Crude Rotation
50 Then Wherefore
.51 Second-Death
52 Carnival of Numbers
54 Love as Love
59 In Nineteen Twenty-Seven

Notes: Published in December, 1928, at 10s. 6d. according to
the *English Catalogue of Books*, but Hugh Ford (H131) reports
it was sold by a London bookseller named Bain at 11s. 6d.
Ford also writes that the Seizin Press hand-set books used
Caslon type and Batchelor hand-made paper. The title page
device, Riding told him, was an "illustration of certain re-
lation-principles" she designed.

SEIZIN ONE

175 numbered copies of this edition have been printed, and this is no. 47

Laura Riding

SEIZIN TWO: AN ACQUAINTANCE WITH DESCRIPTION
BY GERTRUDE STEIN.

SEIZIN THREE: POEMS 1929 BY ROBERT GRAVES.

SEIZIN FOUR: NO TROUBLE BY LEN LYE.

(to follow)

LOVE AS LOVE, DEATH AS DEATH

BY

LAURA RIDING

Printed and published at The Seizin Press
Hammersmith London 1928

Publisher's notice and title page of *Love as Love, Death as Death* (A8)

A9   POEMS: A JOKING WORD   1930

Poems A Joking Word │ by │ Laura Riding │ [publisher's device │
London • Jonathan Cape • Toronto │ 1930

Collation: 8 1/4 x 5 3/4 in., [A]^8 B-K^8 L^7, pp. [1-4] 5-7 [8]
9-22 [23-24] 25-171 [172]. [1]: '*Poems* A Joking Word'. [2]:
blank. [3]: title page. [4]: blank. 5-7: Contents. [8]:
blank. 9-22: Preface. [23]: '*Poems* A Joking Word'. [24]:
blank. 25-171: text. [172]: '*Acknowledgements to* │ *The Hogarth
Press and The Seizin Press* │ *for certain poems here reprinted* │
Printed in Great Britain, in the City of Oxford, at THE ALDEN
PRESS'.

Binding and dust jacket: Beige cloth over boards. Front blank.
Back blind-stamped with publisher's device. Spine printed in
gold: '*POEMS* │ A │ JOKING │ WORD │ [ornament] │ LAURA │ RIDING │
JONATHAN │ CAPE'. Only top edge trimmed.
   Cream dust jacket with black printing on front: 'LAURA
RIDING │ *POEMS* │ A JOKING WORD'. Back cover advertises *Contemporaries and Snobs*, *Anarchism Is Not Enough*, and *A Pamphlet
Against Anthologies*. Inside flap copy: "This is the first
comprehensive collection (1919-1929) of Laura Riding's poems.
It includes the substance not only of *The Close Chaplet* published in 1926 and of *Love as Love, Death as Death*, published
in 1928, but also the deferred *First Poems* announced some
seasons ago; and certain later poems."

Paper: Cream wove paper, including endpapers.

Contents:
 9 Preface
25 Lida
32 Home
33 Incarnations
34 Because I Sit Here So
36 The Mask
37 The Signature
38 Hospitality to Words
39 Room
40 Chloe or....
41 So Slight
42 Take Hands
43 Fragments
47 Chrysalis
48 Yes and No
49 The Tillaquils
51 Fragments from Alastor

Note: Published in July, 1930, at 6s.

A10   FOUR UNPOSTED LETTERS TO CATHERINE   1930

FOUR UNPOSTED LETTERS | TO CATHERINE | BY | *LAURA RIDING* |
HOURS PRESS | *15, Rue Guénégaud* | PARIS

Collation: 7 1/2 x 5 1/2 in., unsigned, pp. [i–vi] 1–50 [51–
52]. [i]: '*FOUR UNPOSTED LETTERS* | *TO CATHERINE* | *COVERS BY*
LEN LYE'. [ii]: blank. [iii]: title page. [iv]: blank.
[v]: '*Dear Gertrude.* | *The function of Opinion is to be that*
which | *does not get posted. Hating Opinion and lov-* | *ing*
All That Gets Posted as you do, you must | *applaud my not*

Front (*left*) and back (*right*) cover of *Four Unposted Letters to Catherine* (A10); design by Len Lye

FOUR UNPOSTED LETTERS
TO CATHERINE

LAURA RIDING

HOURS PRESS
15, Rue Guénégaud
PARIS

Title page of *Four Unposted Letters to Catherine* (A10)

posting these letters, however | *you deplore my writing them.* |
Love, | *Laura.*' [vi]: blank. 1-[51]: text, printed in italic.
[52]: blank. Recto of endpaper: '200 copies of this book |
have been hand-set and | printed by Frazier-Soye | for THE
HOURS PRESS | Each copy signed by the author | This is No
[written] 177 | [signed] Laura Riding'.

Binding: Cream paper over boards. Design printed in gray
tints on front resembles a primitive drawing of an ostrich;
drawing on back suggests a rodent. Brown leather on spine
extends 1/2 in. onto front and back. Spine printed lengthwise
in gold: 'LAURA RIDING 1930 FOUR UNPOSTED LETTERS TO
CATHERINE'. All edges untrimmed.

Paper: Cream wove paper watermarked 'Vidalon' with an insignia
including initials 'IHS'. Same endpapers.

Contents:
1 The First Letter: To Begin With
10 The Second Letter: To Continue to Begin With
23 The Third Letter: To Discuss Learning
35 The Fourth Letter: To Tell About the Muddle

Notes: Published in July, 1930, at 40s. Nancy Cunard describes
the production of this volume in H116. The Hours Press used
Caslon type and Rives paper. Cunard quotes several reviews
which praised the new directness of Riding's style. The letters were addressed to Robert Graves's daughter to encourage
her to resist all the influences that would prevent her from
being herself. The prefatory letter beginning "Dear Gertrude"
alludes to a quarrel between Gertrude Stein and Laura Riding
that estranged them from each other. Riding's letters to
Stein are in the Beinecke Library at Yale.

A11   EXPERTS ARE PUZZLED   1930

[printed in a circle] EXPERTS ARE PUZZLED | LAURA RIDING |
London • JONATHAN CAPE • Toronto

Collation: 8 x 5 1/4 in. [A]^8 B-K^8, pp. [1-4] 5 [6] 7 [8-12]
13-110 [111-112] 113-160. [1]: 'EXPERTS | ARE PUZZLED'. [2]:
'By the Same Author | CONTEMPORARIES AND SNOBS | ANARCHISM IS
NOT ENOUGH | POEMS A JOKING WORD'. [3]: title page. [4]: 'FIRST
PUBLISHED 1930 | JONATHAN CAPE LTD., 30 BEDFORD SQUARE, LONDON |
AND 91 WELLINGTON STREET WEST, TORONTO | JONATHAN CAPE &

EXPERTS ARE PUZZLED

LAURA RIDING

London · JONATHAN CAPE · Toronto

Title page of *Experts Are Puzzled* (A11)

HARRISON SMITH INC. | 139 EAST 46TH STREET, NEW YORK | PRINTED
IN GREAT BRITAIN BY J. AND J. GRAY, EDINBURGH | PAPER SUPPLIED
BY JOHN DICKINSON AND CO. LTD. | BOUND BY NEVETT LTD.' 5-[6]:
Contents. 7: '[7 lines of verse] | [in square brackets] From
Automancy by Lilith Outcome.'. [8]: blank. [9]: 'EXPERTS |
ARE PUZZLED'. [10]: blank. [11]: 'PART I'. [12]: blank.
13-110: text. [111]: 'PART II'. [112]: blank. 113-160: text.

Binding and dust jacket: Beige cloth over boards. Front blank.
Back blind-stamped with publisher's device. Spine printed in
red: 'EXPERTS | ARE PUZZLED | [ornament] | LAURA | RIDING |
JONATHAN CAPE'. Top and fore-edges trimmed.
  Cream dust jacket printed in black. Front flap reads: "The
title of this book is that of the first of the prose pieces of
which it is composed. But it is a title in more than this
merely formal sense. It is a conclusion concerning the fundamental limitations of human intelligence, and this is a book
about intelligence. And yet it is not a dogmatic conclusion.
Indeed, the purpose of the book, in so far as so moderate a
book may be said to have a purpose--is to see how far an un-
puzzled intelligence may go without disrespect to experts, and
how far it can keep within the agreed limitations without
violence to its obsessions. *Miss Banquett, or the Populating
of Cosmania*, is the most elaborate experiment in gentleness in
the book."

Paper: Cream wove paper, including endpapers.

Contents:

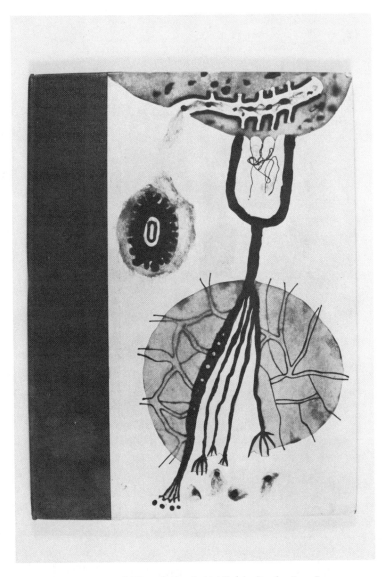

Front cover of *Though Gently* (A12); design by Len Lye

Notes: Published in November, 1930, at 6s. Epigraph attributed to Lilith Outcome introduces pseudonym Riding also used in *Everybody's Letters*. Dust jacket copy illustrates prose style of most of the stories. Using riddles, paradoxes, and parables to "puzzle" the experts, Riding expostulated on a range of subjects, including veiled references to her recent suicide attempt (Easter, 1929).

A12   THOUGH GENTLY   1930

THOUGH | GENTLY | BY | LAURA RIDING | The Seizin Press | Deya, Majorca | 1930

Collation: 11 1/8 x 8 1/4 in., unsigned, pp. [i-iv] 1-29 [30-32]. [i]: 'A SEIZIN'. [ii]: blank. [iii]: title page. [iv]: blank. 1-29: text. [30]: 'There are 200 numbered and signed copies of | Seizin 5 hand-set and hand-printed by ourselves | on hand-made paper--the cover by Len Lye. | NUMBER [written] 130 | [signed] Laura Riding'. [31-32]: blank.

Binding: Cream paper over boards. Design printed in brown tints on both covers is abstract photomontage suggesting a bird-like creature hatching from an egg. Brown cloth on spine extends 2 in. onto front and back. Spine printed in gold lengthwise: 'SEIZIN 5   THOUGH GENTLY   LAURA RIDING'. All edges trimmed.

Paper: Cream laid paper watermarked with a hammer and anvil, a monogram superimposing B and S, and a crest including the words 'BRITISH HAND MADE'. Same endpapers.

Contents:
 1   What Is There to Believe In
 2   Let
 3   Numbers
 4   The Sphinx?, Fancy
 5   The Problem of Evil, Right and Wrong
 6   Ideas and Idea
 7   England and America
 8   The Crowd
10   If a Poem Lasts Twenty-Four Hours

THOUGH GENTLY

BY

LAURA RIDING

The Seizin Press
Deya, Majorca
1930

Title page of *Though Gently* (A12)

THE SPHINX?

An image of meaning as eternally suspended?
Devilishly contrived to stand eternally between
detail and the essential?
But fancy breaks the Sphinx's false spell:
For fancy is a vanity of ripeness in detail
When numbers themselves incline capriciously
Towards finality rather than suspension.

FANCY

10 is the finite of 5.
5 is the infinite of 1.
1 is the repose of 2.
2 is the will of 9.
9 is the question of 3.
3 is the guess of 4.
4 is the patience of 7.
7 is the boldness of 8.
8 is the anxiety of 6.
6 is the foolishness of numbers.

*

Plainly woman tells of man, man of God,
Obscurely God of woman.

Between the word and the world lie
Friendly eternities of soon.

4

THE PROBLEM OF EVIL

The problem of evil is not the problem of
good and evil, but only the problem of evil. In
opposition to good there are evil characters, but
there are not good characters in opposition to
evil. Evil is arguable, but good is not. Therefore
the Devil always wins the argument. And the
inarguability of good is demonstrated in the
plausibility of evil. But what is to become of
the Devil or, to speak accumulatively, the evil
characters, after all the arguments are won? He
must get out of the spotlight of interest, and
yet he has nowhere to go. He must disappear
from himself. He must become commonplace.
Perhaps he devotes himself to an explosive soph-
istry on behalf of good. This is written not in
philosophical but historical speculation. The
poor human figure to which the Devil has at
reduced is present, or was just now.

RIGHT AND WRONG

To be right brings an elation and a depression. The elation is of being right. The
depression is of being right against prevailing
wrong. The fact of confusion breeds in the fact
of clarity a sense of embarrassed irrelevance,
the feeling that to be right is to be violent.
The only justification that wrong ever makes of
itself is the prematurity of right. Wrong is
gentle. It is more pleasant to feel gentle than
violent, and more right-seeming. But what of
being right? Being right comes later, at the
end. If to be right brings a depression, the
depression is a sign by which to know what is
the past.

5

Sample pages of *Though Gently* (A12)

Notes: Published in January, 1931, at 25s., this was the first Seizin Press book published in Majorca. In addition to the titled poems and paragraphs, other passages are untitled, separated only by an asterisk. A Seizin advertisement described the book: it "consists of statements in prose and poetry all leading as gently as possible to annihilation and the rest."

A13   TWENTY POEMS LESS   1930

Twenty Poems Less | *Laura Riding* | *HOURS PRESS* | 15, *Rue Guénégaud, PARIS* | 1930

Collation: 11 x 7 1/2 in., unsigned, pp. [i-iv] 1-33 [34-36]. [i]: '*TWENTY POEMS LESS* | *by* | *Laura Riding* | *Covers* | *by* | *LEN LYE*'. [ii]: blank. [iii]: title page. [iv]: '*CONTENTS*'. 1-33: text. [34]: blank. [35]: '200 COPIES OF THIS BOOK | SET BY HAND AND PRIVATELY | PRINTED ON HAND-PRESS | EACH COPY HAS BEEN | SIGNED BY THE AUTHOR | THIS IS NO [written] 169 | [signed] Laura Riding'. [36]: blank.

Binding: Cream paper over boards printed with photograph of an abstract collage. Front cover includes stones, wood, net, and string arranged to suggest primitive figures. Back cover suggests same arrangement photographed from rear. Brown leather on spine extends 1/2 in. onto front and back. Printed in gold down spine: 'LAURA RIDING   1930   TWENTY POEMS LESS'. Only top edge trimmed.

Paper: White Rives wove paper watermarked 'DALON HAUT' with

an insignia including letters 'IHS', a cross, and three spears
emerging from a heart. Same endpapers.

Contents:
1   As to a Frontispiece
2   Egypt
3   Earth
4   Arithmetic
5   An Opinion
6   There Are as Many Questions as Answers
8   The Fact
9   The Judgement
10 The Way It Is
11 Whose
12 And I
13 We the
15 Now
16 Further Details
18 Or Hello
20 In Memory of Friends
21 An International Hymn
22 Gentle Truth
23 Meaning
25 Then Follows
33 Zero

Notes: Offered in England by Simpkin at 30s. in May, 1931, this
volume was planned as the companion to Robert Graves's *Ten Poems
More.* Nancy Cunard reminisces about her association with
Riding and Graves in H116. The first poem, "As to a Frontispiece," is excluded from the sum of poems because it stands in
place of a picture of the author.

A14   LAURA AND FRANCISCA   1931

LAURA AND FRANCISCA | BY | LAURA RIDING | The Seizin Press |
Deyá, Majorca | 1931

Collation: 11 x 8 in., unsigned, pp. [i-vi] 1-22 [23-26].
[i]: 'A SEIZIN'. [ii]: blank. [iii]: title page. [iv]: blank.
[v]: 'LAURA AND FRANCISCA'. [vi]: blank. 1-22: text. [23]:
blank. [24]: 'NOTE | On page 9 the line | 'The moment for us
to be:' | should read | 'The moment for us to be two:''. [25]:
'There are 200 numbered and signed copies of | Seizin 7 hand-
set and hand-printed by ourselves | on hand-made paper. The

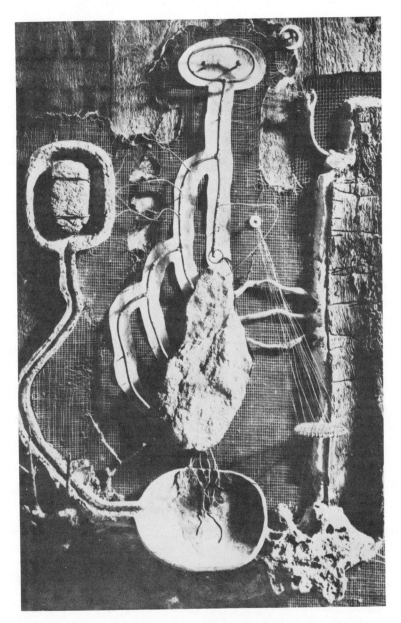

Front cover of *Twenty Poems Less* (A13); design by Len Lye

Twenty

Poems

Less

Laura Riding

HOURS PRESS
15, Rue Guénégaud, PARIS
1930

Title page of _Twenty Poems Less_ (A13)

cover is by Len Lye. | [written] 161 | [signed] Laura Riding'.
[26]: blank.

Binding: Blue paper over boards. Front and back have similar
white line drawings suggesting fantastic creatures. Gray
cloth on spine extends 3/4 in. onto both covers. Spine
printed lengthwise in silver: 'SEIZIN 7   LAURA AND FRANCISCA
LAURA RIDING'. All edges trimmed.

Paper: Cream laid paper watermarked 'GUARRO', with crest between 'A' and 'R'. Same endpapers.

Notes: Published in November, 1931, at 25s. The poem is
divided into 3 parts: I. "The Island, and Here," II. "Francisca,
and Scarcely More," III. "How the Poem Ends." The poem contrasts "Laura" with "Robert": his sensuous pleasures prevent
him from achieving her spiritual unity. She identifies herself
with "Francisca," a village child who teaches her the wisdom of
silence and indifference. Laura's isolation is considered
parallel to that of an island or a poem. A Seizin advertisement called the book "a poem-miniature." Riding described the
cover designs in a letter to Hugh Ford (H131): "a mapping of
interconnected forms and movement-paths that could be thought
of as a microscopic field of natural energy, and on the back
cover, of the play of released forces in spacial extension."

A15   NO DECENCY LEFT   1932

NO DECENCY LEFT | BY | BARBARA RICH | [publisher's device] |
JONATHAN CAPE | THIRTY BEDFORD SQUARE | LONDON

Collation: 7 5/8 x 5 in., [A]^8 B-S^8, pp. [1-8] 9-287 [288].
[1]: 'NO DECENCY LEFT'. [2]: blank. [3]: title page. [4]:
'FIRST PUBLISHED 1932 | JONATHAN CAPE LTD., 30 BEDFORD
SQUARE, LONDON | AND 91 WELLINGTON STREET WEST, TORONTO |
JONATHAN CAPE & HARRISON SMITH, INC. | 139 EAST 46TH STREET,
NEW YORK | PRINTED IN GREAT BRITAIN BY J. AND J. GRAY,
EDINBURGH | PAPER SUPPLIED BY JOHN DICKINSON AND CO. LTD. |
BOUND BY A.W. BAIN AND CO. LTD.' [5]: 'TO | MY PUBLISHER'.
[6]: blank. [7]: 'NO DECENCY LEFT'. [8]: blank. 9-[288]:
text.

Binding: Peach cloth over boards. Front has design of a
crown printed in royal blue. Back blind-stamped with pub-
lisher's device. Spine also printed in blue: 'NO | DECENCY |

Front cover of *No Decency Left* (A15) (peach cloth printed in royal blue)

NO DECENCY LEFT

BY

BARBARA RICH

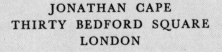

JONATHAN CAPE
THIRTY BEDFORD SQUARE
LONDON

Title page of *No Decency Left* (A15)
with librarian's notation

LEFT | [ornament] | BARBARA | RICH | JONATHAN CAPE'. Top and
fore-edges trimmed.

Paper: Cream wove paper, including endpapers.

Notes: Published in February, 1932, at 7s. 6d. and in a cheap
edition (Half-crown fiction) in March, 1935, at 2s. 6d. In
"Some Autobiographical Corrections of Literary History" (C52),
Riding objects to Graves's identification of "Barbara Rich" as
the pseudonym of the two of them. The terms of her objection,
however, imply that his real offense was in claiming to have
collaborated with her: "Mr. Graves and I knew the authorship
of this book. If he wished to claim collaborative share in it,
that was his business. He had no authority from me for
association of my name with himself as collaborator in that
book: my say as to my relation to that book is my business."
She still does not acknowledge authorship of this novel.
"Barbara Rich" is the name of the heroine. She decides to
make her twenty-first birthday a "really perfect day" only to
discover that the price of pursuing her goal is that she has
"no decency left," but success is what matters for her own
happiness.

A16   THE FIRST LEAF   1933

BY | LAURA RIDING | The Seizin Press | Deyá, Majorca | 1933

Collation: 8 3/4 x 11 in. A single sheet folded twice. Uncut.
Unsigned, unpaged. [1]: title page. [2]: blank. [3]: *THE
FIRST LEAF*'. [3-6]: text. [7-8]: blank.

Binding: Unbound. Tied sheaf.

Paper: Cream laid paper watermarked 'MOLIVELL' and 'GUARRO',
with an upraised left hand between 'A' and 'R', and '1698'
under the hand.

Notes: This poem became Part I of "Disclaimer of the Person,"
which appeared in Riding's *Collected Poems*. "The Second Leaf"
became Part II of the same poem. In spite of the similar
format of the two leaves, the differences in their poetic content are profound.
   The copy at the State University of New York at Buffalo is
in its original presentation envelope and has a strand of red
yarn drawn through the center fold and tied in a bow mid-point
on outer edge.

EVERYBODY'S | LETTERS | *Collected and Arranged by* | LAURA
RIDING | *With an Editorial* | *Postscript* | LONDON | ARTHUR
BARKER LIMITED | 21 GARRICK STREET, COVENT GARDEN

Collation: 8 1/2 x 5 in., [A]^8 B-Q^8, pp. [1-4] 5-7 [8] 9 [10]
11-93 [94] 95-175 [176] 177 [178] 179-227 [228] 229 [230] 231-
253 [254-256]. [1]: 'EVERYBODY'S LETTERS'. [2]: blank. [3]:
title page. [4]: 'FIRST PUBLISHED IN 1933 | *Copyright*
Reserved | *Made and Printed in Great Britain by* | *Hazell,*
Watson & Viney, Ltd., London and Aylesbury'. 5-6: Foreword.
7: Contents. [8]: '*Every letter is printed exactly as found*'.
9: '*PART I* | THE BRITISH SPIRIT'. [10]: blank. 11-92: text.
93: '*PART II* | THE UNIVERSAL SPIRIT'. [94]: blank. 95-175:
text. [176]: blank. 177: '*PART III* | THE AMERICAN SPIRIT'.
[178]: blank. 179-227: text. [228]: blank. 229: 'EDITORIAL
POSTSCRIPT'. [230]: blank. 231-253: text. [254-256]: blank.

Binding and dust jacket: Black cloth over boards. Front has
white paper label (2 1/4 x 3 1/2 in.) printed in blue. A
single rule border encloses: 'EVERYBODY'S LETTERS | *Collected*
and Arranged by | LAURA RIDING | [rule] | ARTHUR BARKER LTD.,
LONDON'. White label (2 1/4 x 1 1/4 in.) on spine also printed
in blue with single rule border: 'EVERY- | BODY'S | LETTERS |
LAURA RIDING'. Back blank. Top edge colored deep blue. Top
and fore-edges trimmed.

Dust jacket black with light blue lettering. Copy on front
flap reads: "These letters have not been chosen as examples of
good writing or of bad writing or of foolish writing. They
have not, indeed, been 'chosen' at all, but rather gathered in
accidentally from the world's exchange of affectionately's and
very sincerely's—a bundle of letters from Harry in Sydney to
Cecil in Iraq, and from Paul Cousins at Wallingford to his dear
Chesney friends (American Express Co., Paris), and from Mummy
to Morgan, and from Monty to Darling.... And so here are as
many 'real' letters as the editor could decently avail herself
of, printed without considerations of style, authorial importance, or the importance of the places, persons or situations
to which they refer."

Paper: Cream wove paper, including endpapers.

Contents:

Notes: Published at 10s. 6d. in February, 1933, this book pur-
ports to be a collection rather than a creation by the author.
But the British Museum Catalogue appends "[or rather, writter]
by" Laura Riding to its entry. Textual evidence also suggests
Riding was more than an editor. The letters are linked to form
an epistolary portrait of a group of friends, not unlike the
circle surrounding Riding and Graves in Majorca. For example,
"Lilith Outcome" and "Hubey Pitt" wrote a book called *Modern
Literary Conventions*. "Lilith Outcome" was also the author of
the epigraph from *Automancy* used in *Experts Are Puzzled*. In "Son
Autobiographical Corrections of Literary History" (C52), Riding
identifies "Lilith" as herself and "Cyril" as Norman Cameron.
Further, she accuses Norman Cameron of republishing the letters
he had written to her in his *The Collected Poems of Norman
Cameron (1905-1953)*, intro. by Robert Graves (London: The
Hogarth Press, 1957). She writes: "In the Introduction there
are ten pages of transcription of letters described by Mr.
Graves as written to myself and him by Norman Cameron when he
was in Nigeria as an Education Officer. These letters are
taken from a collection of actual letters, by many, edited
and published by me with an 'Editorial Postscript' in 1933
under the title *Everybody's Letters*; the letters were not
textually tampered with by me, but names of persons and places
I took care to change."

A18   THE LIFE OF THE DEAD   1933

THE | LIFE OF THE DEAD | BY | LAURA RIDING | With Ten
Illustrations by John Aldridge | *Engraved on wood by* | R.J.
BEEDHAM | ARTHUR BARKER LTD. | 21, GARRICK STREET, COVENT
GARDEN | LONDON, W.C. 2

Collation: 12 1/2 x 9 3/4 in., unsigned, pp. [1-4] 5 [6] 7-8
[9-10] 11-14 [15-16] 17-18 [19-20] 21-22 [23-24] 25-26 [27-28]
29-30 [31-32] 33-34 [35-36] 37-38 [39-40] 41-44 [45-46] 47-48
[49-52]. [1]: 'THE | LIFE OF THE DEAD'. [2]: blank. [3]:
title page. [4]: blank. 5: '*EXPLANATION*'. [6]: blank. 7-8:
text. [9]: plate. [10]: blank. 11-14: text. [15]: plate.
[16]: blank. 17-18: text. [19]: plate. [20]: blank. 21-22:
text. [23]: plate. [24]: blank. 25-26: text. [27]: plate.
[28]: blank. 29-30: text. [31]: plate. [32]: blank. 33-34:

text. [35]: plate. [36]: blank. 37-38: text. [39]: plate. [40]: blank. 41-44: text. [45]: plate. [46]: blank. 47-48: text. [49]: plate. [50]: blank. [51]: 'Two hundred numbered copies of "The | Life of the Dead" have been printed on | Basingwerk Parchment in 14-point Pastonchi | by Messrs. Hazell, Watson & Viney, Ltd. | Each copy is signed by the Author and the | Illustrator. | [written] 57 | [signed] Laura Riding | [signed] John Aldridge'. [52]: blank.

Binding: Heavy brown paper. Front has beige label (3 1/2 x 4 1/4 in.) printed in black. A double rule border encloses: 'THE | LIFE OF THE DEAD | BY | LAURA RIDING | *With Ten Illustrations by* | JOHN ALDRIDGE'. Back blank. Top and fore-edges trimmed.

Paper: White wove paper watermarked 'BASINGWERK PARCHMENT'. Brown wove endpapers similar to covers.

Notes: Although no date appears in the volume, the book was published in September, 1933, at 35s. The author's "Explanation" accounts for its unusual format: a French poem, an English translation, and an illustration for each of 10 conceptions. She chose to write in French because she was reluctant to use English, a language which "makes things so real," for her "outrageous subject."

A19   POET: A LYING WORD   1933

POET: A LYING WORD | by | LAURA RIDING | LONDON | ARTHUR BARKER LTD. | 1933

Collation: 8 1/2 x 5 1/2 in., [A]^8 B-K^8, pp. [i-iv] v-vii [viii] [1-2] 3-31 [32-34] 35-64 [65-66] 67-89 [90-92] 93-119 [120-122] 123-149 [150-152]. [i]: 'POET: A LYING WORD'. [ii]: blank. [iii]: title page. [iv]: '*First published* 1933 | *Printed in Great Britain by Sherratt & Hughes, at the* | *St Ann's Press, Manchester*'. v-vii: Contents. [viii]: blank. [1]: 'PART I | SHREWD WINTER, AND THE LAST: | THE NEXT YEAR STANDS STILL'. [2]: blank. 3-31: text. [32]: blank. [33]: 'PART II | SPRING HOLDS THE PRESENT BACK'. [34]: blank. 35-64: text. [65]: 'PART III | SUMMER NEVER SO EXTREME, NOR AGAIN'. [66]: blank. 67-89: text. [90]: blank. [91]: 'PART IV | AUTUMN'S LAST WORD: GRIEF, SPITE AND | THE INVOLUNTARY SMILE OF DEATH'. [92]: blank. 93-119: text. [120]: blank. [121]: 'PART V | FAILURE OF SEASON'. [122]: blank. 123-[150]: text. [151-152]: blank.

Binding: Black cloth over boards. Front printed in gold:
'POET: A LYING WORD | LAURA RIDING'. Spine printed in gold:
'POET: | A | LYING | WORD | LAURA | RIDING | BARKER'. All
edges trimmed. Back blank. Top edge colored steel blue.

Paper: Cream laid paper. Cream wove endpapers.

Contents:

Notes: Published in December, 1933, at 6s., this book expresses Riding's fury at the recalcitrance of words in
yielding truth. The title suggests the theme of the new
poems in this volume and anticipates her later rejection of
poetry. But before abandoning poetry altogether, she attained
a level of truth-telling described in the preface to her
Collected Poems and illustrated in her final section of that
book, "Poems Continual." The question mark after "Who," the
poem listed on p. 16, appears only in the Contents.

*A20   PICTURES   1933

PICTURES | [rule] | LAURA RIDING

Collation: 7 1/2 x 5 in., unsigned, unpaged. [1-8]: text.

Binding: Paper cover serves as title page and endpaper. Back
blank. Top and bottom edges trimmed, fore-edge untrimmed.
6d. stamp seals front and back covers at mid-point of fore-
edge.

Paper: Cream laid paper.

Notes: Alan Clark describes this pamphlet in his checklist
(A43). He says it was unofficially issued by the Seizin Press
in London in 1933. Hugh Ford, quoting a letter from the
author (H131), notes that the pamphlet was similar to her
article "Picture-Making" in *Epilogue* I (A27).

A21   14A   1934

LAURA RIDING & GEORGE ELLIDGE | 14A | [double rule] | *ARTHUR BARKER* | *21 GARRICK STREET* | *LONDON W.C. 2*

Collation: 7 3/8 x 4 3/4 in., [A]^8 B–T^8, pp. [1–7] 8–302 [303–304]. [1]: '14A'. [2]: blank. [3]: title page. [4]: 'FIRST PUBLISHED IN 1934 | PRINTED IN GUERNSEY, C.I., BRITISH ISLES, | BY THE STAR AND GAZETTE COMPANY LTD.' [5]: 'No character in this story has any | existence in fact'. [6]: blank. [7]–302: text. [303–304]: blank.

Binding: Blue cloth over boards. Front and back blank. Spine printed in gold: '14A | LAURA RIDING | & | GEORGE | ELLIDGE | BARKER'. Top and fore-edges trimmed.

Paper: Cream wove paper, including endpapers.

Notes: Published in February, 1934, at 7s. 6d., this novel in dialogue form recounts intrigues involving a group of people in an apartment numbered 14A. The characters resemble the circle including Riding, Graves, and Nancy Nicholson in St. Peter's Square, Hammersmith, in the late 1920's. In his autobiography, Frank O'Connor identifies one of the characters, "Handy Andy," as himself (H113). Other characters are very similar to Riding, Graves, Nicholson, Gertrude Stein. Riding attempted to suppress the novel by omitting it from every bibliographical or biographical account she authorized until 1976.

A22   AMERICANS   1934

AMERICANS | [rule] | [red design of American eagle bending a bar in its claws] | [rule] | BY LAURA RIDING | PRIMAVERA | 1934

Collation: 9 3/8 x 6 1/4 in., unsigned, pp. [1–7] 8–28 [printed in red in upper fore-edge]. [1]: 'AMERICANS'. [2]: blank. [3]: title page. [4]: 'Two hundred numbered copies printed by Ward | Ritchie, August 1934, in the U.S.A. The title-page | device is an adaptation of a heraldic eagle for | the United States invented by Szu kal ski. Copy- | right 1934 by Laura Riding. [written in red pencil] 37'. [5]: Foreword. [6]: blank. [7]–28: text.

Binding: Buff paper over boards printed with all-over pattern of blue stars at 1 in. intervals. Red cloth on spine extends 1/4 in. onto covers. Narrow buff label (2 1/4 in. long) on spine printed in blue lengthwise: 'AMERICANS [ornament] Riding'. Only top edge trimmed.

Paper: Cream laid paper watermarked 'JCA [script] France'. Same endpapers.

Notes: Priced at $2.50, this volume was so beautifully produced that Riding expressed regret in *Focus* III, p. 8, that she had sent Ward Ritchie such an "ill-tempered deliberately shabby" poem.

A23   FOCUS I   1935

FOCUS | I.

Collation: 8 1/2 x 6 1/2 in., unsigned, pp. 1-12. 1: 'JANUARY'. 1-12: text.

Binding: Paper cover also serves as title page and endpaper. Back blank. Sheets folded in half and center-stapled once. All edges trimmed.

Paper: Cream wove paper.

Contents:
   1 Letter from Honor Wyatt
   2 Letter from Gordon Glover
   3 Letter from James Reeves
   4 Letter from Robert Graves
   5 Letter from Karl Goldschmidt
   7 Letter from Laura Riding
  11 Letter from John Aldridge

Notes: No publication or printing notice. No price. *Focus* was planned as a periodical which would publish personal statements from contributors who, for the most part, knew each other. It was distributed privately among friends. Riding's letter discusses her current reading, a book about women as people she wanted to write, her progress on a Dictionary of Related Meanings she had begun the year before, and her hopes for *Focus*.

A24   FOCUS II   1935

FOCUS | II. 1935

Collation: 8 1/2 x 6 1/2 in., unsigned, pp. 1-24. 1: 'FEBRUARY-
MARCH'. 1-23: text. [24]: blank.

Binding: Paper cover also serves as title page and endpaper.
Back blank. Sheets folded in half and center-stapled once.
All edges trimmed.

Paper: Cream wove paper.

Contents:
 1 Letter from Honor Wyatt
 2 Letter from Gordon Glover
 4 Letter from James Reeves
 5 Letter from Thomas Matthews
 7 Letter from Julie Matthews
 8 Letter from John Aldridge
11 Letter from Harold Edwards
12 Letter from Karl Goldschmidt
18 Letter from Laura Riding
22 "A Portrait," by John Cullen

Notes: Riding writes about Thalia-Thalius, an androgynous
character she based on the muse of comedy; cats; the prepara-
tion of *Focus and Epilogue*; and current work including poems,
a story, a "Letter to Myself," and "a strange big-money
emprise. "

A25   THE SECOND LEAF   1935

BY | LAURA RIDING | The Seizin Press | Deyá, Majorca | 1935

Collation: 11 x 8 3/4 in. A single sheet folded twice.
Uncut. Unsigned, unpaged. [1]: title page. [2]: blank.
[3]: '*THE SECOND LEAF*'. [3-6]: text. [7-8]: blank.

Binding: Unbound. Tied sheaf.

Paper: Cream laid paper watermarked 'MOLIVELL' and 'GUARRO',
with an upraised left hand between 'A' and 'R', and '1698'
under the hand.

Notes: This poem became Part II of "Disclaimer of the Person," which appeared in Riding's *Collected Poems*. "The First Leaf" became Part I of the same poem.

A26 FOCUS III 1935

FOCUS | III. 1935

Collation: 8 1/2 x 6 1/2 in., unsigned, pp. 1-40. 1: 'APRIL-MAY'. 1-40: text.

Binding: Paper cover also serves as title page and endpaper. Back blank. Sheets folded in half and center-stapled once. All edges trimmed.

Paper: Cream wove paper.

Contents:
```
 1  Letter from James Reeves
 7  Letter from Laura Riding
15  Letter from John Aldridge
17  Letter from Honor Wyatt
20  Letter from Karl Goldschmidt
23  Letter from Robert Graves
28  Letter from Gordon Glover
31  Letter from Mary Phillips
32  Letter from Laura Riding
```

Notes: Riding's first letter discusses other contributors; *Americans*; current work including the translation of *Almost Forgotten Germany* (A30); *Epilogue*; her "storybook"; plans for "little books of moral purport, called 'Seizin Homilies' and now and again a Leaf"; and the death of T.E. Lawrence. Her second letter discusses letters from other contributors; quotes Graves's parody of "The boy stood on the burning deck"; and discusses a letter from Michael Roberts concerning her participation in his anthology.

A27 EPILOGUE I 1935

EPILOGUE | A Critical Summary | *Volume I--Autumn* 1935 | [rule] | *Editor:* | Laura Riding | *Assistant-Editor:* | Robert

Graves │ [rule] │ Contributors to this Issue: │ [names
printed in two columns] MADELEINE VARA   LAURA RIDING │ JAMES
REEVES   ROBERT GRAVES │ THOMAS MATTHEWS   HONOR WYATT │ JOHN
CULLEN   JOHN ALDRIDGE │ LEN LYE   WARD HUTCHINSON │ [rule] │
THE SEIZIN PRESS · DEYA MAJORCA │ AND │ CONSTABLE & CO LTD │
LONDON

Collation: 8 1/2 x 5 1/2 in., [A]^8 B–Q^8, pp. [i–iv] v [vi]
1–245 [246–248]. 4 leaves of plates on coated stock printed
on recto inserted before p. 219 and 1 leaf before p. 237.
[i]: 'EPILOGUE'. [ii]: blank. [iii]: title page. [iv]:
'MADE & PRINTED IN GREAT BRITAIN │ BY THE WHITEFRIARS PRESS
LTD. │ LONDON & TONBRIDGE'. v: Contents. [vi]: Epigraph of
three lines of verse, unsigned and untitled. 1–245: text.
[246]: Advertisement: *'For Autumn Publication* │ [rule] │
THE MOON'S NO FOOL │ by THOMAS MATTHEWS │ A MISTAKE SOMEWHERE │
ANONYMOUS │ THE NATURAL NEED │ Poems │ by JAMES REEVES │
PROGRESS OF STORIES │ by LAURA RIDING │ THE SEIZIN PRESS ·
DEYA MAJORCA │ and │ CONSTABLE & CO LTD │ London'. [247–248]:
blank.

Binding: Beige paper over boards. Front cover printed in
black: 'Twice a Year' in upper left corner, 'Volume I' in
upper right. Center: 'EPILOGUE │ A CRITICAL SUMMARY │
[Design resembling the etchings by John Aldridge for *The
Life of the Dead* depicts a blank scroll unwinding from middle
of a curtained classical proscenium arch. Left of the arch is
a stage backdrop simulating a brick wall. To the right is a
spear leaning against a fortified building. Clouds float
above.] │ AUTUMN 1935 │ Laura Riding [swung dash] Editor │
Robert Graves [swung dash] Associate Editor │ THE SEIZIN
PRESS . DEYA MAJORCA │ AND │ CONSTABLE & CO. LTD. │ LONDON │
Seven Shillings and Sixpence net'. Back blank. Spine printed
in black: 'EPILOGUE │ A │ CRITICAL │ SUMMARY │ I │ AUTUMN │
1935'. All edges trimmed.

Paper: Cream laid paper, including endpapers.

Contents:
   1 Preliminaries: Laura Riding
   6 The Idea of God: Thomas Matthews and Laura Riding
  55 Poems: Thomas Matthews
  60 The Cult of Failure: Laura Riding and Madeleine Vara
  87 A Poem–Sequence: Robert Graves
  93 Germany: Laura Riding, John Cullen, Madeleine Vara
 130 Poems: John Cullen
 134 An Address to an International Audience: Madeleine Vara
 144 Poems and Poets: Laura Riding

Twice a Year   Volume I

EPILOGUE

A CRITICAL SUMMARY

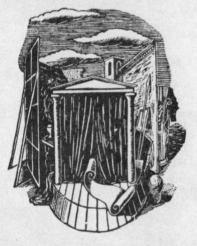

AUTUMN 1935

Laura Riding - Editor

Robert Graves - Associate Editor

THE SEIZIN PRESS . DEYA MAJORCA

AND

CONSTABLE & CO. LTD.

LONDON

Seven Shillings and Sixpence net

Front of *Epilogue* I (A27)

Notes: Epilogue was issued in book format though it appeared
periodically. The intention was to publish regularly yet
assure the permanence of a bound book. *Epilogue* was not to
be discarded when finished but was to become a permanent
possession because its purpose was "truth-telling," to
examine important subjects and articulate what was "final"
about them. Only three issues appeared. *The World and Ourselves* was called *Epilogue* IV, but its format was entirely
different from the preceding issues.

  Riding's poems are "A Letter to Any Friend," "Be Grave,
Woman," "The Need to Confide," "The Reasons of Each,"
"Divestment of Beauty."

A28   FOCUS IV   1935

FOCUS | IV. 1935

Collation: 8 1/2 x 6 1/2 in., unsigned, pp. 1-64. 1: 'DECEMBER
1935'. 1-64: text.

Binding: Paper cover also serves as title page and endpaper.
Back blank. Sheets folded in half and center-stapled once.
All edges trimmed.

Paper: Cream wove paper.

Contents:
  1   Laura and Robert: Majorcan Letter, 1935
 10   James
 15   Gordon
 18   Robert: Christmas
 19   Tom

23 Honor
26 Laura: Christmas
26 John
29 Robert
33 James: Christmas
34 Laura
39 Tom's Likes
40 Robert's Likes
43 James' Likes
45 Gordon's Like
46 Lucie's Likes
47 John's Like
47 Honor's Likes
48 Karl
51 Laura

Notes: "Majorcan Letter, 1935" is a topical, satirical poem
which was offered to Denys Kilham Roberts and John Lehmann
for *The Year's Poetry 1934*, but they refused it because it
was too long and the authors would not shorten it, Riding
explains in her last entry. Instead, the anthology included
"Midsummer Duet, 1934" by Riding and Graves. *Focus* IV also
included Christmas poems by Graves, Riding, and James Reeves.
Riding introduces her plan for "Likes" with personal examples,
and in the last letter she reflects on the past year.

A29   PROGRESS OF STORIES   1935

PROGRESS | OF | STORIES | by | LAURA RIDING | THE SEIZIN
PRESS • DEYÁ MAJORCA | and | CONSTABLE & CO LTD | London

Collation: 7 1/4 x 5 3/4 in., [A]^8 B-U^8 X^{10}, pp. [1-4] 5 [6]
7-17 [18-20] 21-105 [106-108] 109-194 [195-196] 197-288 [289-
290] 291-318 [319-320] 321-339 [340]. [1]: 'PROGRESS OF
STORIES'. [2]: blank. [3]: title page. [4]: 'PUBLISHED
BY | *The Seizin Press • Deyá Majorca* | and | *Constable and
Company Ltd* | LONDON | • | *The Macmillan Company* | *of Canada,
Limited* | TORONTO | *First published* 1935 | Made in Great
Britain. Printed by Sherratt & Hughes, | at the St. Ann's
Press, Manchester'. 5: Contents. [6]: blank. 7-17: Preface.
[18]: blank. [19]: 'I | STORIES OF LIVES'. [20]: blank.
21-105: text. [106]: blank. [107]: 'II | STORIES OF IDEAS'.
[108]: blank. 109-194: text. [195]: 'III | NEARLY TRUE
STORIES'. [196]: blank. 197-288: text. [289]: 'IV | A CROWN
FOR HANS ANDERSEN'. [290]: blank. 291-318: text. [319]:
'V | MORE STORIES'. [320]: blank. 321-[340]: text.

PROGRESS OF STORIES

LAURA RIDING

DEIX

SEIZIN PRESS
AND
CONSTABLE

Dust jacket of *Progress of Stories* (A29)

Binding and dust jacket: Green cloth over boards. Front and back blank. Spine printed in black: 'PROGRESS | OF | STORIES | [ornament] | LAURA | RIDING | [publisher's device] | SEIZIN PRESS | AND | CONSTABLE'. All edges trimmed.

Buff dust jacket printed in red (see illustration). Back advertises other Seizin-Constable books: *Epilogue* I, *The Natural Need* by James Reeves, *The Moon's No Fool* by Thomas Matthews, and *A Mistake Somewhere*, Anonymous. Description of book on front flap: "This collection of stories, beginning in a matter-of-fact narrative vein, takes us in rising degrees of mysteriousness to unaccustomed levels of narrative.... It is the communication of such a story-feeling that has been the author's object, rather than, merely, to ring fictional changes on ordinary events and people. Stories are sometimes more than the strange incidents and characters that compose them: they represent, more essentially, a feeling of curiosity and expectation which we must suppress in our daily prearranged lives, and which the conventional material of stories satisfies only temporarily."

Paper: Cream laid paper. Cream wove endpapers.

Contents:

Notes: Priced at 7s. 6d., this book's publication date listed in the *English Catalogue of Books* is January, 1936. Although the

Cumulative Book Index, 1933-37 lists a Random House edition at
$2.50, Random House verifies that a separate edition was
never published. Random House and the Seizin Press did,
however, reach an agreement for the distribution of Seizin
books in the United States.
   A reprint edition was published by Books for Libraries
Press (Freeport, N.Y.) in 1971.

A30   ALMOST FORGOTTEN GERMANY   1936

ALMOST FORGOTTEN | GERMANY | by | GEORG SCHWARZ | Translated
by | LAURA RIDING and ROBERT GRAVES | [publisher's device] |
THE SEIZIN PRESS · DEYÁ MAJORCA | AND | CONSTABLE & CO.,
LTD. | London

Collation: 7˙3/8 x 4 3/4 in., [A]^{16} B-I^{16}, pp. [i-iv] v [vi]
vii-viii 1-278 [279-280]. Frontispiece: informal photograph
printed on verso of coated stock facing title page, between
p. [ii] and p. [iii]. [i]: 'ALMOST FORGOTTEN GERMANY'. [ii]:
Advertisement for Seizin-Constable books including *Epilogue*,
Progress of Stories, *The Natural Need* (James Reeves), *A Mistake Somewhere* (Anonymous), *The Moon's No Fool* (Thomas
Matthews). [iii]: title page. [iv]: 'PUBLISHED BY | *The
Seizin Press · Deyá Majorca* and *Constable and Company Ltd.* |
LONDON | · | *The Macmillan Company* | *of Canada Limited* |
TORONTO | *First published* 1936 | *Printed in Great Britain* |
by Western Printing Services | *Ltd., Bristol*'. v: Contents.
[vi]: blank. [vii-viii]: Foreword. 1-278: text. [279-280]:
blank.

Binding and dust jacket: Dark orange cloth over boards. Front
and back blank. Spine printed in black: 'ALMOST | FORGOTTEN |
GERMANY | GEORG SCHWARZ | Translated by | LAURA RIDING |
and | ROBERT GRAVES | [publisher's device] | SEIZIN PRESS |
AND | CONSTABLE'. All edges trimmed.
   Orange dust jacket printed in black, white, and red. Front
design shows a painter in monk's robe superimposed on a map
of Germany. Back advertises *Epilogue*, *Convalescent Conversations* (Madeleine Vara), *Antigua, Penny, Puce* (Robert Graves),
A Trojan Ending, *Subjects of Knowledge*. Copy on front flap
reads, in part: "A retired art-dealer, now expatriated, tells
the story of his varied early life in what has come to be
thought of as 'Old Germany.'"

Paper: Cream wove paper, including endpapers.

Notes: Published in April, 1936, at 7s. 6d. Although the *Cumulative Book Index, 1933-37* lists a Random House edition at $2.50 and Alan Clark's Checklist (A43) includes it, Random House verifies that a separate edition was never published. Random House, however, distributed this book in the United States. A memo dated 1 February 1937 in the Random House files lists sales and inventories of five Seizin Press books including *Progress of Stories* and *Almost Forgotten Germany*.

The publisher's device on the title page was designed by Karl Goldschmidt, Riding told Hugh Ford (H131). It employs "the antique insignia of the village of Deyá."

A31   CONVALESCENT CONVERSATIONS   1936

CONVALESCENT | CONVERSATIONS | BY | MADELEINE VARA | [publisher's device] | THE SEIZIN PRESS DEYÁ MAJORCA | AND | CONSTABLE & CO LTD | London

Collation: 7 1/4 x 5 in., [A]^8 B-I^8, pp. [i-iv] 1-139 [140]. [i]: 'CONVALESCENT CONVERSATIONS'. [ii]: Advertisement for Seizin-Constable Books including *Epilogue*, *Progress of Stories*, *The Natural Need* (James Reeves), *A Mistake Somewhere* (Anonymous), *The Moon's No Fool* (Thomas Matthews). [iii]: title page. [iv]: 'PUBLISHED BY | *The Seizin Press* • *Deyá Majorca* | and | *Constable and Company Ltd.* | LONDON | • | *The Macmillan Company* | *of Canada Limited* | TORONTO | *First published* 1936 | PRINTED IN GREAT BRITAIN BY | MACKAYS LIMITED, CHATHAM'. 1-[140]: text.

Binding: Gray cloth over boards. Front and back blank. Spine printed in black: 'CONVA- | LESCENT | CONVER- | SATIONS | MADELEINE | VARA | [publisher's device] | SEIZIN | AND | CONSTABLE'. All edges trimmed.

Paper: Cream wove paper, including endpapers.

Notes: Published in July, 1936, at 5s., this novel in dialogue form is set in a nursing home where Eleanor and Adam are convalescing under the care of Miss Kenwood, the matron. It is described in a Seizin-Constable advertisement at the State University of New York at Buffalo: "A book of informal dialogue between two intelligent invalids bent on not falling in love. On the nursinghome veranda each morning they discuss air-mindedness, virginity, the uses of old people, how fashions

start, mental pictures of God, feminism. And sometimes Nurse
Davies joins in, and the austere Matron unbends; and Mrs.
Lyley, a fellow-patient, will probably succeed in her plot
for a conventional ending."

Riding acknowledges the pseudonym in "Some Autobiographical
Corrections of Literary History" (C52).

A32   EPILOGUE II   1936

EPILOGUE | A Critical Summary | *Volume II--Summer* 1936 |
[rule] | *Editor*: | Laura Riding | *Associate Editor*: | Robert
Graves | [rule] | Contributors to this Issue: | [names printed
in two columns] ALAN HODGE   HONOR WYATT | JAMES REEVES
KENNETH ALLOTT | MADELEINE VARA   LAURA RIDING | WARD
HUTCHINSON   ROBERT GRAVES | KATHERINE BURDEKIN   GORDON
GLOVER | [rule] | THE SEIZIN PRESS · DEYA MAJORCA | AND |
CONSTABLE & CO LTD | LONDON

Collation: 8 1/2 x 5 1/2 in., [A]^8 B-Q^8 R^1, pp. [i-iv] v [vi]
1-251 [252]. [i]: 'EPILOGUE'. [ii]: Advertisement: 'SEIZIN-
CONSTABLE BOOKS | [rule] | ALMOST FORGOTTEN GERMANY | by
GEORG SCHWARZ | *Translated by Laura Riding and Robert Graves* |
A retired art-dealer, now expatriated, tells the story of his
varied | early life in what has come to be thought of as "Old
Germany." | A frank, odd book. | CONVALESCENT CONVERSATIONS |
by MADELEINE VARA | A book of informal dialogue between two
intelligent invalids bent | on not falling in love. | ANTIGUA,
PENNY, PUCE | a Novel by ROBERT GRAVES | This postage-stamp
of curious history and doubtful ownership is the | occasion
of a bitterly fought feud between a successful actress and
her | brother, an unsuccessful novelist. After a tragi-comic
parade of the | viler human passions, the stamp and the
quarrel are eventually be- | queathed to the next generation. |
A TROJAN ENDING | a Novel by LAURA RIDING | There was something
mysterious about the story of the siege and fall | of Troy
that has made it excite the imagination of all succeeding
times. | This novel explores the mystery and finds a clue in
the opposition of | Trojan and Greek temperaments. The
author has reconstructed | the story with sympathy and
eloquence. | SUBJECTS OF KNOWLEDGE | A series of simply
written books, suitable for schoolroom or general | reading,
in which the subjects are treated both historically and
critically | by a committee of Seizin authors. | SCHOOLS: A
summary of the history of schools and educational | ideas
throughout the world. | POETS: How there came to be professional

poets, the develop- | ment of various types of poems, the
attitude to poets and poetry | during different periods of
history.' [iii]: title page. [iv]: 'PUBLISHED BY | *The
Seizin Press . Deyâ Majorca* | and | *Constable and Company
Ltd.* | LONDON | • | *The Macmillan Company* | *of Canada Limited* |
TORONTO | *First published* 1936 | MADE AND PRINTED IN GREAT
BRITAIN | BY THE WHITEFRIARS PRESS LTD. | LONDON AND
TONBRIDGE'. v: Contents. [vi]: Epigraph of three lines of
verse, unsigned and untitled. 1-[252]: text. [252]: colophon.

Binding: Light green paper over boards. Front cover printed
in black: 'Twice a Year' in upper left corner, 'Volume II' in
upper right. Center: 'EPILOGUE | A CRITICAL SUMMARY | [Design
of Volume I repeated--a blank scroll unwinds from center of a
curtained classical proscenium arch. Left of arch is a stage
backdrop simulating a brick wall. At right a spear leans
against a fortified building. Clouds float above.] | SUMMER
1936 | Laura Riding [swung dash] Editor | Robert Graves
[swung dash] Associate Editor | THE SEIZIN PRESS • DEYA
MAJORCA | AND | CONSTABLE & CO. LTD. | LONDON | *Seven Shillings
and Sixpence net*'. Back blank. Spine printed in black:
'EPILOGUE | A | CRITICAL | SUMMARY | II | SUMMER | 1936'.
All edges trimmed.

Paper: Cream laid paper, including endpapers.

Contents:

Note: Riding's poems are "On a New Generation," "Because of
Clothes," and "The Wages of Eloquence."

A33   EPILOGUE III   1937

EPILOGUE │ A Critical Summary │ *Volume III--Spring* 1937 │
[rule] │ *Editor:* │ Laura Riding │ *Associate Editor:* │ Robert
Graves │ [rule] │ Contributors to this Issue: │ [names printed
in two columns, except last is centered] MADELEINE VARA
ALAN HODGE │ NORMAN CAMERON   HONOR WYATT │ SALLY GRAVES
KARL GOLDSCHMIDT │ BASIL TAYLOR   ROBIN HALE │ LUCIE BROWN
JOHN ALDRIDGE │ WILLIAM ARCHER   HARRY KEMP │ LAURA RIDING
ROBERT GRAVES │ WARD HUTCHINSON   THOMAS MATTHEWS │ JAMES
REEVES │ [rule] │ THE SEIZIN PRESS . DEYA MAJORCA │ AND │
CONSTABLE & CO LTD ┊ LONDON

Collation: 8 1/2 x 5 1/2 in., [A]^8 B-L^8 M-N^{10} O-Q^8, pp. [i-iv]
v [vi] 1-257 [258]. 4 leaves of plates on coated stock bear
photographs of paintings on recto, inserted before p. 191.
[i]: 'EPILOGUE'. [ii]: 'IN APOLOGY │ EPILOGUE III would
normally have appeared in the │ autumn of 1936. Events in
Spain delayed its publication. │ Apologies are offered to
booksellers and readers for this │ apparent breach of
editorial good faith. The same causes │ are responsible for
the delay of other scheduled Seizin Press │ works: see
announcement at the end of this volume.' [iii]: title page.
[iv]: PUBLISHED BY │ *The Seizin Press • Deyá Majorca* │ and │
Constable and Company Ltd. │ LONDON │ • │ *The Macmillan
Company* │ *of Canada Limited* │ TORONTO │ *First published* 1937 │
MADE AND PRINTED IN GREAT BRITAIN │ BY THE WHITEFRIARS PRESS
LTD. │ LONDON AND TONBRIDGE'. v: Contents. [vi]: Epigraph
of three lines of verse, untitled and unsigned. 1-[258]:
text. [258]: colophon.

Binding: Light red paper over boards. Front cover printed in
black: 'Twice a Year' in upper left, 'Volume III' in upper
right. Center: 'EPILOGUE │ A CRITICAL SUMMARY │ [Design of
Volumes I and II repeated--a blank scroll unwinds from center
of a curtained classical proscenium arch. Left of arch is a
stage backdrop simulating a brick wall. At right a spear leans
against a fortified building.] │ SPRING 1937 │ Laura Riding

[swung dash] Editor | Robert Graves [swung dash] Associate
Editor | THE SEIZIN PRESS . DEYA MAJORCA | AND | CONSTABLE &
CO. LTD. | LONDON | *Seven Shillings and Sixpence net* | PRINTED
IN GREAT BRITAIN'. Back blank. Spine printed in black:
'EPILOGUE | A | CRITICAL | SUMMARY | III | SPRING | 1937'.
All edges trimmed.

Paper: Cream laid paper.   Cream wove endpapers.

Contents:

Notes: Riding's poems include "I Remember," "The Forgiven
Past," "The Cycle of Industry," "When Love Becomes Words."
The article on "Politics and Poetry" was expanded by Harry
Kemp for *The Left Heresy in Literature and Life* (A38).   The
announcement promised in the Apology does not appear.

A34   A TROJAN ENDING   1937

a. First British edition

A TROJAN ENDING | *By* | LAURA RIDING | [publisher's device] |
THE SEIZIN PRESS--DEYÁ MAJORCA | AND | CONSTABLE & COMPANY
LTD | LONDON

Collation: 7 7/8 x 5 in., [a]^4 b-c^8 B-Z^8 AA-DD^8 EE^6, pp. [extra
sheet] [i-viii] ix-xxix [xxx] [1-2] 3-58 [59-60] 61-132 [133-
134] 135-201 [202-204] 205-275 [276-278] 279-357 [358-360]
361-436 [437-oversize sheet]. Recto of extra sheet: 'A TROJAN
ENDING'. Verso: blank. [i]: title page. [ii]: 'PUBLISHED
BY | *Constable and Company Ltd.* | LONDON | • | *The Macmillan
Company* | *of Canada, Limited* | TORONTO | • | *First Published in*
1937 | PRINTED IN GREAT BRITAIN BY THE WHITEFRIARS PRESS LTD. |
LONDON AND TONBRIDGE'. [ii]: blank. [iii]: 'TO KATHARINE
WEST'. [iv]: blank. [v]: Contents. [vi]: blank. [vii]:
'[epigraph of 3 lines] | CHAUCER, *Troilus and Criseyde.*'
[viii]: blank. ix-xxviii: Preface. xxix: Contents. [xxx]:
blank. [1]: 'BOOK ONE | FROM THE SCAEAN TOWER'. [2]: blank.
3-58: text. [59]: 'BOOK TWO | IN HELEN'S CHAMBER'. [60]:
blank. 61-132: text. [133]: 'BOOK THREE | THE TRUCE'. [134]:
blank. 135-201: text. [202]: blank. [203]: 'BOOK FOUR |
WINTER'. [204]: blank. 205-275: text. [276]: blank. [277]:
'BOOK FIVE | WITH THE SPEED OF SPRING'. [278]: blank. 279-
357: text. [358]: blank. [359]: 'BOOK SIX | PEACE'. [360]:
blank. 361-432: text. 433-436: 'INDEX OF PRINCIPAL
CHARACTERS'. [437]: fold out map on 16 1/2 in. sheet: 'THE
TROJAN WAR: GREECE AND ASIA MINOR IN THE EARLY TWELFTH CENTURY
B.C.'

Binding: Black cloth over boards. Front and back blank.
Spine printed in red: 'A | TROJAN | ENDING | LAURA | RIDING |
SEIZIN | CONSTABLE'. Top edge colored red. All edges trimmed.

Paper: Cream wove paper, including endpapers and map.

Contents:
ix   Author's Preface
 1   Book I: From the Scaean Tower
59   Book II: In Helen's Chamber
133 Book III: The Truce
203 Book IV: Winter
277 Book V: With the Speed of Spring
359 Book VI: Peace
433 Index of Principal Characters

Notes: Published in March, 1937, at 8s. 6d. and issued by
Macmillan in Toronto at $2.75. The Contents on p. xxix relists
titles and pages of sections.

b. *First American edition*

A TROJAN ENDING | [mauve design of concentric circles] | BY
LAURA RIDING

Collation: 8 1/4 x 5 1/2 in., unsigned, pp. [i-ix] x-xxviii
[xxix-xxx] [1] 2-56 [57] 58-128 [129] 130-195 [196-197] 198-
267 [268-269] 270-347 [348-349] 350-421 [422] 423-426 [427-
428]. [i]: blank. [ii]: in mauve: '[publisher's device] |
RANDOM HOUSE | NEW YORK'. [iii]: title page. [iv]:
'COPYRIGHT, 1937, BY RANDOM HOUSE, INC. | A Seizin Press Book.
First Printing. Designer: | Ernst Reichl. Manufactured in
the United | States of America by H. Wolff, New York.' [v]:
'TO KATHARINE WEST'. [vi]: blank. [vii]: '[epigraph of 3
lines] | CHAUCER, TROILUS AND CRISEYDE'. [viii]: blank. [ix]-
xxviii: Preface. [xxix]: Contents. [xxx]: blank. [1]: 'BOOK
I • FROM THE SCAEAN TOWER'. 2-56: text. [57]: 'BOOK II IN
HELEN'S CHAMBER'. 58-128: text. [129]: 'BOOK III THE TRUCE'.
130-195: text. [196]: blank. [197]: 'BOOK IV WINTER'. 198-
267: text. [268]: blank. [269]: 'BOOK V • WITH THE SPEED OF
SPRING'. 270-347: text. [348]: blank. [349]: 'BOOK VI PEACE'.
350-421: text. [422]: blank. 423-426: 'INDEX OF PRINCIPAL
CHARACTERS'. [427-428]: blank.

Binding: Gray cloth over boards. Front repeats title page
design of concentric circles in black and white. Back blank.
Spine repeats title page design in black on a white band above
and below the following printed in black: 'A TROJAN | ENDING |
LAURA RIDING | RANDOM HOUSE'. Top edge colored mauve. All
edges trimmed.

Paper: Cream wove paper, including endpapers.

Contents:
    1 Book I; From the Scaean Tower
   57 Book II; In Helen's Chamber
  129 Book III; The Truce
  197 Book IV; Winter
  269 Book V; With the Speed of Spring
  349 Book VI; Peace

Notes: Published in August, 1937, at $2.50. Variant binding
is red cloth over boards. Front design in black. Spine omits
design.

A35   COLLECTED POEMS   1938

a. First British edition

COLLECTED POEMS | [rule] | LAURA RIDING | [publisher's device] |
CASSELL | AND COMPANY LIMITED | LONDON, TORONTO, MELBOURNE AND
SYDNEY

Collation: 8 1/2 x 5 1/2 in., [a]^8 b^6 A–Z^8 2A–2G^8, pp. [i–iv]
v [vi] vii–xiii [xiv] xv–xxviii [1–2] 3–60 [61–62] 63–149 [150–
152] 153–260 [261–262] 263–367 [368–370] 371–418 [419–420]
421–422 [423–424] 425–432 [433–434] 435–438 [439–440] 441–442
[443–444] 445–448 [449–450] 451–456 [457–458] 459–462 [463–
464] 465–466 [467–468] 469–472 [473–474] 475–477 [478–480].
[i]: 'COLLECTED POEMS'. [ii]: blank. [iii]: title page.
[iv]: '*Collected Poems* is published by | arrangement with the
SEIZIN PRESS | *First published* . . 1938 | Printed in Great
Britain by T. and A. CONSTABLE LTD. | at the University Press,
Edinburgh | F.438'. v: 'The Poems in this edition are collected
from the | following books:–– | THE CLOSE CHAPLET (Hogarth
Press). | LOVE AS LOVE, DEATH AS DEATH (Seizin Press). | POEMS:
A JOKING WORD (Jonathan Cape Ltd.). | THOUGH GENTLY (Seizin
Press). | TWENTY POEMS LESS (Hours Press). | POET: A LYING
WORD (Arthur Barker Ltd.). | [rule] | VOLTAIRE (Hogarth
Press). | LAURA AND FRANCISCA (Seizin Press). | THE LIFE OF
THE DEAD (Arthur Barker Ltd.). | [rule] | EPILOGUE, Volumes I,
II and III (Seizin Press and | Constable & Co.) | and from
hitherto unpublished work. | Thanks are given to the Publishers
mentioned | above for their kind permission to reprint | poems
first published by them.' [vi]: blank. vii–xiii: Contents.
[xiv]: blank. xv–xxviii: 'To the Reader'. [1]: 'POEMS OF
MYTHICAL OCCASION'. [2]: blank. 3–60: text. [61]: 'POEMS OF
IMMEDIATE OCCASION'. [62]: blank. 63–149: text. [150]: blank.
[151]: 'POEMS OF FINAL OCCASION'. [152]: blank. 153–260:
text. [261]: 'POEMS CONTINUAL'. [262]: blank. 263–367: text.
[368]: blank. [369]: 'HISTORIES'. [370]: blank. 371–418:
text. [419]: blank. [420]: illustration ["Le Coeur sec"].
421–422: text. [423]: blank. [424]: illustration ["Les Trois
Ames des Morts"]. 425–432: text. [433]: illustration ["Le
Théâtre de Mortjoy"]. [434]: blank. 435–438: text. [439]:
illustration ["La Transformation de Romanzel"]. [440]: blank.
441–442: text. [443]: blank. [444]: illustration ["La Naissance
des Bébés Morts"]. 445–448: text. [449]: blank. [450]: illustration ["A l'intérieur de la ville: de jour"]. 451–456:
text. [457]: illustration ["A l'intérieur de la Ville: de
Nuit"]. [458]: blank. 459–462: text. [463]: illustration
["Le Banquet des Morts"]. [464]: blank. 465–466: text. [467]:

blank. [468]: illustration ["La Musée de l'Aube"]. 469–472: text. [473]: blank. [474]: illustration ["La Déesse qui Plaisante"]. 475–477: text. [478–480]: blank.

Binding and dust jacket: Green cloth over boards. Front and back blank. Spine printed in gold. A wreath encloses: 'COLLECTED POEMS | · | Laura | Riding | CASSELL'. Top edge colored yellow. All edges trimmed.
  Buff dust jacket printed in black and orange. Front flap advertises *Lives of Wives*. Back flap advertises Robert Graves's *Collected Poems*. Back describes Riding's work.

Paper: Cream wove paper, including endpapers.

Contents:

Notes: Published in September, 1938, at 15s. Dust jacket copy
describes Riding's work: "We must read them [these poems] in
relation to one another to appreciate the large coherence of
thought behind them. Then, instead of assuming a mysterious
personality at work in intellectual isolation, we recognize
that here is a complete range of poetic experience controlled
with sensitive wisdom.... They are, moreover, very consciously
the work of a woman, introducing into poetry energies without
which it is no more than 'a tradition of male monologue', not
a living communication."

The description of *Lives of Wives* is also noteworthy because
the final volume did not follow the original plan: "The book
begins with the story of Amytis, wife of Cyrus of Persia, and
includes, in its review of 2,500 years of wifedom, the wives
of Aristotle, Herod the Great, Cicero, Mohammed, Charlemagne,
Canute, Baldwin of Bourg, James I of Aragon, Frans Hals,
Molière, Fox, Emerson, Karl Marx, Garibaldi." Only the first
three wives were included.

b. First American edition

COLLECTED POEMS | [rule] | LAURA RIDING | [publisher's device] |
RANDOM HOUSE | NEW YORK

Collation: Identical to British edition.

Binding and dust jacket: Royal blue cloth over boards. Front
and back blank. Spine displays title in box (2 1/8 x 1 3/8 in.)
defined by deeper blue background and gold border. Publisher's
device--a house--rests on top of the box. Gold printing in
box: 'COLLECTED | POEMS | [ornament] | LAURA | RIDING | RANDOM
HOUSE'. Top edge colored gray. All edges trimmed.

Buff dust jacket printed in dark blue and black. Copy on
flap describes book. Back lists Random House poetry.

Paper: Cream wove paper, including endpapers.

Note: Priced at $4.00.

A36   THE WORLD AND OURSELVES   1938

THE WORLD | AND OURSELVES | Laura Riding | To relieve this
world unhappiness--to have | a world worthy of our minds--we
must | ourselves be worthy of our minds, we our- | selves must
be the solution. Peace does | not come before order but after
it. Order | is not achieved by taking action but by | taking
thought. There is a happy world | outside when there are
minds | at work inside. | 1938 | CHATTO & WINDUS | LONDON

Collation: 8 1/2 x 5 1/2 in., [A]^6 B-Z^8 AA-KK^8 LL^{10}, pp. [i-iv]
v-xi [xii] [1-2] 3-44 [45-46] 47-129 [130-132] 133-220 [221-
222] 223-367 [368-370] 371-529 [530-532]. [i]: 'THE WORLD AND
OURSELVES'. [ii]: 'This represents the fourth volume of the
literary | series *Epilogue*. I have thought it important at
this | time to suspend the work of general criticism begun in |
the first three volumes, and to make a special inquiry | into
the state of the world to-day in relation to our- | selves.
I hope soon to be able to renew the original | programme with
Epilogue V. | L.R.' [iii]: title page. [iv]: 'PUBLISHED BY |
Chatto & Windus | LONDON | [ornament] | The Macmillan Company |
of Canada, Limited | TORONTO | PRINTED IN GREAT BRITAIN | ALL
RIGHTS RESERVED'. v-viii: Contents. ix-xi: Foreword. [xii]:
blank. [1]: 'PART I. INTRODUCTION'. [2]: blank. 3-44: text.
[45]: 'PART II. THE ANSWERS | MALENESS AND FEMALENESS'. [46]:
blank. 47-129: text. [130]: blank. [131]: 'PART III. THE
ANSWERS | THE REALISTIC APPROACH'. [132]: blank. 133-220:
text. [221]: 'PART IV. THE ANSWERS | BEGINNING FROM THE
INSIDE'. [222]: blank. 223-367: text. [368]: blank. [369]:
'PART V. CONCLUSION | *Recommendations and Resolutions*'. [370]:
blank. 371-529: text. [530]: blank. [531]: colophon. [532]:
blank.

Binding and dust jacket: Maroon cloth over boards. Front and
back blank. Spine printed in gold: 'THE | WORLD AND |
OURSELVES | [decorative swung dash] | Laura Riding | CHATTO |
AND WINDUS'. Top edge colored maroon. Top and fore-edges
trimmed.

  Dust jacket brown with beige letters, but colors reversed
on front: title and author printed in brown inside a beige
circle. Copy on inside flap describes book: "The author
addressed a carefully worded letter to some four hundred
people, and she quotes, classifies and comments upon a selection of the answers she received. These include letters from
people of widely different ages, occupations and temperaments--
some famous, some not--and together present an extremely in-
teresting cross-section of intelligent opinion on a subject of
immense importance: namely, the position of sensible men and
women to-day, wanting to live a peaceful, civilised existence,

in a world which has become steadily more and more disordered
and less and less peaceful. What, if anything, can such
people do?"

Paper: Cream laid paper. Cream wove endpapers.

Contents:

450   (9) Companies of Friends as the Basis of Self-
                Government
467   (10) Not to Apply Past Solutions to Present Problems
476   (11) Indications for a New Moral Law
484   (12) Redeeming Intelligent People from Vulgarity of
                Behaviour and Thought
497   (13) The Proper Attitude and Approach to the Multi-
                tudes and Their Problems
509   (14) How to Speak Purely, in a Way to Avoid Fallacies
                of Language and Mediocrity of Thought
519   II. Resolutions 1-27

Notes: Published in November, 1938, at 15s. In 1969 Riding
wrote a new preface, "For Later Readers," for the University
Microfilms edition, and Northwestern University holds the
corrected typescript (F10). Cornell University also lists a
manuscript copy of the 1969 Preface (F5).

*A37   THE COVENANT OF LITERAL MORALITY   1938

THE COVENANT OF | LITERAL MORALITY | Protocol I | THE SEIZIN
PRESS | 1938

Collation: 8 1/2 x 5 1/2 in., unsigned, pp. [1] 2-16. [1]:
title page. 2-15: text. 16: 'Those whom Laura Riding has
consulted in drawing up this | Protocol are: [26 names in two
columns, last name centered] JOHN ALDRIDGE   DOROTHY
HUTCHINSON | LUCIE BROWN   WARD HUTCHINSON | GEORGE BUCHANAN
ALIX KEMP | MARY BUCHANAN   HARRY KEMP· | NORMAN CAMERON   LEN
LYE | GORDON GLOVER   ALBERT MILLS | ROBERT GRAVES   MARY
PHILLIPS | SALLY GRAVES   BERYL PRITCHARD | LIDDELL HART
DAVID REEVES | ETHEL HERDMAN   JAMES REEVES | ALAN HODGE
DOROTHY SIMMONS | JACK HOLMES   MONTAGUE SIMMONS | WINIFRED
HOLMES   JANE THOMPSON | HONOR WYATT | [rule] | The whole of
this document is copyrighted in the name of Laura Riding. |
Reproduction of any part of it is forbidden. | PRINTED IN GREAT
BRITAIN | BY WESTERN PRINTING SERVICES LTD., BRISTOL'.

Binding: Faded blue gray paper covers. Front printed in black:
'THE COVENANT OF | LITERAL MORALITY | Protocol I | THE SEIZIN
PRESS | 1938'. Loose sheet inserted: '*PRELIMINARY QUESTIONS* |
To be addressed to prospective endorsers. If the answer to
each | *question is not 'Yes', the Protocol itself should not*
be shown to | *them, and the matter dropped.* | DO YOU AGREE: |
[5 questions follow]'. Back blank. All edges trimmed.

Paper: Cream wove paper.

Contents:
2   The Judgment of Evil
13 Explanation
14 Prescriptions

Notes: Privately printed, this pamphlet was intended to be
circulated privately among people likely to agree with its
principles. The "Prescriptions" include the provision that
no endorser may make a copy of the Protocol and new endorsers
must apply for copies directly to the Honorary Secretary,
Norman Cameron. This Protocol preceded the one T.S. Matthews
describes in his autobiographies (H104, H152).

A38   THE LEFT HERESY IN LITERATURE AND LIFE   1939

THE LEFT HERESY IN | LITERATURE AND LIFE | BY | HARRY KEMP,
LAURA RIDING | AND OTHERS | [publisher's device] | METHUEN
PUBLISHERS LONDON | ESSEX STREET STRAND W.C.2

Collation: 7 1/4 x 4 3/4 in., π^4 [1]^8 2-17^8, pp. [i-iv] v [vi]
vii-viii [1-2] 3-62 [63-65] 66-120 [121-122] 123-176 [177-178]
179-212 [213-214] 215-254 [255-257] 258-270 [271-272]. [i]:
'THE LEFT HERESY IN | LITERATURE AND LIFE'. [ii]: blank.
[iii]: title page. [iv]: *'First published in 1939* | PRINTED
IN GREAT BRITAIN'. v: Foreword. [vi]: blank. vii-viii:
Contents. [1]: *'SECTION ONE* | ANALYSIS OF THE LEFT EMOTIONAL |
BACKGROUND'. [2]: blank. 3-62: text. [63]: *'SECTION TWO* |
ANALYSIS OF THE LEFT INTELLECTUAL BACKGROUND'. [64]: blank.
[65]-120: text. [121]: *'SECTION THREE* | ANALYSIS OF THE LEFT
HUMAN BEING'. [122]: blank. 123-176: text. [177]: *'SECTION
FOUR* | THE WITHERING AWAY'. [178]: blank. 179-212: text.
[213]: *'SECTION FIVE* | THE REAL ISSUES'. [214]: blank. 215-
254: text. [255]: *'SECTION SIX* | THE POLITICAL PAST'. [256]:
blank. [257]-270: text. [271]: blank. [272]: colophon.

Binding and dust jacket: Orange cloth over boards. Front and
back blank. Spine printed in red: *'THE LEFT* | *HERESY* | *In
Literature* | *and Life* [ornament] | *HARRY KEMP,* | *LAURA
RIDING* | *and others* | *METHUEN'*. All edges trimmed.
   Dust jacket has black lettering over red and white design
depicting hammer and sickle emblem. Description of book on
front flap: "Mr. Harry Kemp is a poet, and was once a Communist.
His part in the collaboration is based on the experience of

having been a Left, obliged to identify himself with theories
that denied the values he subscribed to as a poet--and with
people whose behaviour and 'ideals' were untidy and ambiguous.
Miss Laura Riding has brought to the book not only a poet's
breadth of view, but that power of clarifying fundamentals
which has come to be increasingly associated with her name."

Paper: Cream wove paper. White wove endpapers.

Contents:

Notes: Published in May, 1939, at 7s. 6d. but raised to 8s. 6d.
The Foreword indicates the first four sections "were written
in close consultation with Laura Riding; and many passages in

the book are directly by her." The last two sections appeared
in *Epilogue* III as "Politics and Poetry" by Laura Riding,
Robert Graves, Alan Hodge, and Harry Kemp.

  Reprints were issued by Folcroft Library Editions (Folcroft,
Pa.) in 1974; and Norwood Editions (Norwood, Pa.) in 1977.

A39   LIVES OF WIVES   1939

a. First British edition

LIVES OF WIVES | *By* | LAURA RIDING | [publisher's device] |
CASSELL | *and Company Limited* | London, Toronto, Melbourne |
and Sydney

Collation: 8 1/2 x 5 1/2 in., A-U^8 X^2, pp. [1-4] 5 [6] 7-8
[9-10] 11-73 [74-76] 77-204 [205-206] 207-323 [324]. [1]:
'LIVES OF WIVES'. [2]: *By the same Author* | COLLECTED POEMS |
THE WORLD AND OURSELVES | A TROJAN ENDING | PROGRESS OF
STORIES'. [3]: title page. [4]: '*First published* . 1939 |
Printed in Great Britain by T. and A. CONSTABLE LTD. | at the
University Press, Edinburgh | F. 539'. 5: Foreword. [6]:
blank. 7-8: Contents. [9]: 'I | A PERSIAN LADY | AND HER
CONTEMPORARIES | [ornament]'. [10]: blank. 11-73: text.
[74]: blank. [75]: 'II | MACEDONIAN TIMES | [ornament]'.
[76]: blank. 77-204: text. [205]: 'III | NEW WAYS IN
JERUSALEM | [ornament]'. [206]: blank. 207-323: text. [324]:
blank.

Binding and dust jacket: Green cloth over boards. Spine
printed in gold: 'LIVES | OF WIVES | [ornament] | LAURA |
RIDING | CASSELL'. Front and back blank. All edges trimmed.
  Buff dust jacket printed in black and sienna. Front flap
advertises *Collected Poems*, quoting Humbert Woolfe in the *Observer*.

Paper: Cream wove paper, including endpapers.

Contents:
      I A Persian Lady, and Her Contemporaries
  11   1 The Medes and the Persians
  15   2 The Rise of Cyrus, Husband of Amytis
  33   3 The Defeat of Croesus
  48   4 The Capture of Babylon
  62   5 The Death of Cyrus

Notes: Published in October, 1939, at 12s. 6d. Foreword explains the title reflects that "the principal male characters are here written of as husbands rather than as heroes."

b. First American edition

LIVES OF WIVES | *By* | LAURA RIDING | [publisher's device] | RANDOM HOUSE | NEW YORK

Collation: Identical to British edition.

Binding and dust jacket: Brown cloth over boards. Front and back blank. Spine displays a black rectangle (2 3/4 x 1 1/8 in.) with silver border. Publisher's device--a house--rests on rectangle. Silver printing in box: 'LIVES | OF | WIVES | [ornament] | LAURA | RIDING | [ornament] | RANDOM | HOUSE'. Top edge colored black. All edges trimmed.
  Buff dust jacket printed in black and yellow.

Paper: Identical to British edition.

Note: Priced at $2.50.

a. First British edition

LAURA RIDING | SELECTED POEMS: | IN FIVE SETS | FABER AND
FABER | London

Collation: 7 1/4 x 4 7/8 in., [A]^8 B-F^8, pp. [1-6] 7-9 [10] 11-
17 [18] 19-94 [95-96]. [1]: 'LAURA RIDING | *Selected Poems:* |
In Five Sets'. [2]: blank. [3]: title page. [4]: '*First
published in 1970* | *by Faber and Faber Limited* | *24 Russell
Square London WC 1* | *Printed in Great Britain by* | *Robert
MacLehose and Co Ltd* | *The University Press Glasgow* | *All
rights reserved* | *SBN 571 091288* | *Copyright 1938 Laura
Riding* | *This edition © by Laura (Riding) Jackson 1970* |
CONDITIONS OF SALE | *This book is sold subject to the condition
that it shall not, by way of* | *trade or otherwise, be lent,
re-sold, hired out or otherwise circulated* | *without the
publisher's prior consent in any form of binding or cover* |
*other than that in which it is published and without a similar
condition* | *including this condition being imposed on the
subsequent purchaser*'. [5]: 'To Patricia Butler, | sure
friend to the end, and beyond, | who forwarded this book with |
glad feeling as she put her desk | in final order.' [6]: blank.
7-9: Contents. [10]: blank. 11-17: Preface. [18]: blank.
19-94: text. [95-96]: blank.

Binding: Paper covers. Front printed in black on bands of light
blue and orange separated by a white strip: 'LAURA | RIDING |
Selected | POEMS: | in Five Sets'. White printing on black
strip along fore-edge: 'FABER paper covered EDITIONS'. Back
advertises other Faber paper-covered editions. Spine extends
colored bands of front cover and has black printing on blue and
orange, white letters on black lengthwise: 'LAURA RIDING |
SELECTED POEMS | FABER'. Copy inside front cover describes the
occasion of this book: "Laura Riding's poems have been unavail-
able for many years since she has been unwilling to allow them
to appear in anthologies. She has made this selection herself
and has written an important preface in which she explains her
attitude to her work." All edges trimmed.

Paper: Cream wove paper. No endpapers.

Contents:

Notes: Published in June, 1970, at 9s. Although the preface states the text is that of Riding's *Collected Poems* except for the correction of misprints and a few verbal changes, the revisions are extensive. Riding offers an explanation for her renunciation of poetry as the result of her belief that she had reached its limit and judges her own poems to be "of the first water as poetry."

b. First American edition

LAURA RIDING | SELECTED POEMS: | IN FIVE SETS | [publisher's device] | W·W·NORTON & COMPANY·INC· | NEW YORK

Collation: 7 3/4 x 5 in., unsigned, pp. [1-6] 7-9 [10] 11-17 [18] 19-94. [1]: 'LAURA RIDING | *Selected Poems:* | *In Five Sets*'. [2]: blank. [3]: title page. [4]: 'COPYRIGHT 1938 LAURA RIDING | This edition copyright © 1970 by Laura (Riding) Jackson | First published in 1970 by Faber & Faber Limited | First American edition published 1973'. Advertisement for Norton books, ISBN for cloth and paper editions, printed in U.S.A. [5]: 'To *Patricia Butler* (my English agent) who, sure friend to the | end, and beyond, forwarded this book with glad feeling | as she put her desk in final order. And, *Charles Monteith* | friend to the book in its English publication | (with others of Faber & Faber). | And to *Sonia Raiziss* (American writer, editor), who, | long devoted to my poems, was the first in later time to write | feelingly on them. And, *Michael Kirkham* (English critic), | who, after her, wrote courageously, on them.' [6]: blank. 7-9: Contents. [10]: blank. 11-17: Preface. [18]: blank. 19-94: text.

Binding and dust jacket: Brown cloth over boards. Front and back blank. Spine printed in silver lengthwise: 'RIDING [ornament] SELECTED POEMS: IN FIVE SETS   NORTON'. All edges trimmed.

Dust jacket design by Nancy Earle: white printing on brown and light blue abstract pattern. Front and back flaps describe Riding's career: "Her aim, which drew associates, was 'to clarify a norm of generally applicable values, by which a moral identity could be established between the poetic and the more casual areas of articulate expression.'"

Paper: Cream wove paper. White wove endpapers.

Contents: Identical to British edition.

Note: Published in 1973 at $6.95.

c. American paper edition

Identical to cloth edition, except binding is paper. Front repeats design of dust jacket. Back summarizes Riding's career and quotes Robert Fitzgerald's praise. Extra sheet at end of book. Priced at $1.95.

A41   THE TELLING   1972

a. First British edition

Laura (Riding) Jackson | THE TELLING | UNIVERSITY OF LONDON | THE ATHLONE PRESS | 1972

Collation: 8 1/2 x 5 1/2 in., unsigned, pp. [i-vi] 1-4 [5] 6 [7-8] 9-56 [57-58] 59-80 [81-82] 83-185 [186]. [i]: 'THE TELLING'. [ii]: 'To Schuyler, my husband, my partner in | the endeavor to take words, and oneself, | further--and, now, to outlive death's long | moment... | and to my mother and my father, who | imparted to me a durable sense of the | further'. [iii]: title page. [iv]: *Published by* | THE ATHLONE PRESS | UNIVERSITY OF LONDON | *at* 4 *Gower Street London wcl* | *Distributed by* | *Tiptree Book Services Ltd, Tiptree, Essex* | *U.S.A. and Canada* | *Humanities Press Inc* | *New York* | © *Laura (Riding) Jackson 1972* | 0 485 11137 3 | *Printed in Great*

Britain by | WILLIAM CLOWES & SONS, LIMITED | *London, Beccles and Colchester'*. [v]: Contents. [vi]: blank. 1-4: *'Nonce Preface'*. [5]: blank. 6: 'OUTLINE'. [7]: 'THE TELLING'. [8]: blank. 9-56: text. [57]: 'PREFACE FOR A SECOND | READING'. [58]: blank. 59-80: text. [81]: 'SOME AFTER-SPEAKING: | PRIVATE WORDS'. [82]: blank. 83-185: text. [186]: blank.

Binding and dust jacket: Blue cloth over boards. Front and back blank. Spine printed in gold lengthwise: '(RIDING) | JACKSON THE TELLING | [publisher's device]'. All edges trimmed.
   White dust jacket printed in gray and purple. Front repeats the title in gray 11 times, in purple once. Author's name also appears in purple. Front flap describes book and summarizes Riding's career. Copy reads, in part: "This short work outlines with great clarity and beauty the view that the significance of life lies in consciousness of existence as shared by all living beings, past and present. In a complementary sense it is concerned with the general function of language as the articulation of our humanness and the truth-function of that."

Paper: White wove paper, including endpapers.

Contents:

1	Nonce Preface
6	Outline
7	The Telling
57	Preface for a Second Reading
81	Some After-Speaking: Private Words
83	1 An Invitation
85	2 The Idea of Rebeginnings
108	3 Extracts from Communications
147	4 Some Notes, Enlarging on Some Features of the Text

Note: Published in October, 1972, at £3.00.

b. First American edition

Laura (Riding) Jackson | THE TELLING | Harper & Row, Publishers | New York Evanston San Francisco London

Collation: 8 x 5 1/2 in., unsigned, pp. [i-vi] [1] 2-4 [5] 6 [7-8] 9-56 [57-58] 59-80 [81-82] 83-185 [186]. [i]: 'THE TELLING'. [ii]: *'Also by Laura (Riding) Jackson:* | Poetic Work (Collections) | POEMS: A JOKING WORD | POET: A LYING WORD | COLLECTED POEMS | SELECTED POEMS | Criticism and Commentary | CONTEMPORARIES AND SNOBS | ANARCHISM IS NOT

ENOUGH | FOUR UNPOSTED LETTERS TO CATHERINE | EPILOGUE (*Editor,
Commentator*) | THE WORLD AND OURSELVES (*Editor, Commentator*) |
Fiction | PROGRESS OF STORIES | A TROJAN ENDING | LIVES OF
WIVES'. [iii]: title page. [iv]: 'The main essay of *The
Telling* was first published in *Chelsea*, 1967. The | book was
originally printed in Great Britain by the Athlone Press of
the | University of London.' Copyright notice. 'Published
simultaneously in Canada by Fitzhenry & Whiteside | Limited,
Toronto.' [v]: Contents. [vi]: 'To Schuyler, my husband, my
partner in | the endeavor to take words, and oneself, | further--
and, now, to outlive death's long | moment... | and to my
mother and my father, who | imparted to me a durable sense of
the | further'. [1]-4: '*Nonce Preface*'. [5]: blank. 6:
'OUTLINE'. [7]: 'THE TELLING'. [8]: blank. 9-56: text.
[57]: 'PREFACE FOR A SECOND | READING'. [58]: blank. 59-80:
text. [81]: 'SOME AFTER-SPEAKING: | PRIVATE WORDS'. [82]:
blank. 83-185: text. [186]: printer's numerals.

Binding and dust jacket: Yellow cloth over boards. Front lower
fore-edge stamped in gold with publisher's device. Back blank.
Brown cloth on spine extends 1 3/4 in. onto front and back.
Spine printed in gold lengthwise: 'Laura (Riding) Jackson
THE TELLING   Harper & Row'. Only top edge trimmed.
   Yellow dust jacket printed in black and blue over design of
flowers in brown. Front and back flaps describe book and
author's career. Copy reads, in part: "Both in what she calls
the 'core-part' of the book and the supplements, there is much
that has a profound importance in our situation: a view of the
nature of women that is different from the traditional, the
'liberal,' and the 'liberated' stance; a unique view of poetry
and its limitations; a treatment of the appeal of myth in
modern literature; a new position on the subject of the spiritual nature of existence."

Paper: White wove paper. Brown wove endpapers.

Contents: Identical to British edition.

Notes: Published in September, 1973, at $6.95. Riding hand-
corrected p. [iv] of the numbered series of 100 to read main
"portion" instead of main "essay."

*A42   FROM THE CHAPTER 'TRUTH' IN RATIONAL MEANING: 1975
            A NEW FOUNDATION FOR THE DEFINITION OF WORDS

[purple] From The Chapter 'Truth' in | [red] Rational Meaning: |
[red] A New Foundation For | [red] The Definition Of Words |
[purple] *(Not Yet Published)* | [purple] by Laura (Riding)
Jackson | [purple] & Schuyler B. Jackson | [purple publisher's
device] | [purple] PRIAPUS PRESS 1975

Collation: 8 1/2 x 5 3/4 in., unsigned, unpaged. [1]: title
page. [2]: blank. [3]: paragraph defining language, signed
'*L.J.*'. [4]: blank.

Binding: Glossy white paper covers. Front repeats printing
and colors of title page. Back blank. Inside back cover
printed in purple: '*Copyright Laura (Riding) Jackson | and
Schuyler B. Jackson 1975 | EDITED, HAND-SET AND PRINTED BY
JOHN COTTON | 45 Copies For Friends Of | THE PRIAPUS PRESS |
37, Lombardy Drive, Berkhamsted, Herts., England.* | Press
device by Rigby Graham'. All edges trimmed.

Paper: White wove paper.

Note: The British Library holds a copy of this pamphlet.

A43   IT HAS TAKEN LONG--   1976

CHELSEA 35 | It Has Taken Long-- | [slanted to upper fore-edge]
FROM THE WRITINGS OF | [facsimile signature] Laura (Riding)
Jackson | [rule]

Collation: 8 1/2 x 5 1/2 in., unsigned, pp. [1-9] 10-20 [21]
22-79 [80-81] 82-159 [160-161] 162-189 [190-191] 192-226 [227]
228-239 [240-244]. [1-2]: blank. [3]: 'SELECTIONS | LAURA
(RIDING) JACKSON'. [4]: 'Author's Note on Copyright | All
rights reserved, for both unpublished and | published material
presented in this issue. A por- | tion of the published
material has suffered the | indignity of capture and subjection
to the form of | literary piracy known as reprinting. But all
the | components of my selection for this issue are | integrally
part of it. The reproduction in any | manner of any of these
without my approval will | be regarded as a serious
infringement. | L.(R.)J.' [5]: '*This collection is dedicated
to Susan Morris, a | perfect friend, who has helped me prepare
it, and | much else, for publication, benignly treating my* |

work and myself as one. | L.(R.)J.' [6]: 'Publication of this
issue | has been made possible by a grant from the |
Coordinating Council of Literary Magazines | made through
funds received from the | *National Endowment for the Arts* and
the | *New York State Council on the Arts*'. [7]: 'CHELSEA |
EDITOR | sonia RAIZISS | *ASSOCIATE EDITORS* | helene DWORZAN |
rose GRAUBART | brian SWANN | *ASSISTANTS TO THE EDITOR* | david
HIRSH | barbara PENTRE | CHELSEA is published by Chelsea
Associates, Inc. | [subscription rates, editorial address,
copyright notice, terms for submissions, disclaimer of opinions
expressed by contributors] 1976'. [8-9]: Contents. 10-11:
'A Word from the Guest Editor'. 12: *'FOREWORD'*. 13-14:
'INTRODUCTORY'. 15-20: text. [21]: 'PART ONE | LANGUAGE AND
LITERATURE'. 22-79: text. [80]: blank. [81]: 'PART TWO |
STORY'. 82-159: text. [160]: blank. [161]: 'PART THREE |
THE AUTHORIAL EXPERIENCE'. 162-189: text. [190]: blank.
[191]: 'PART FOUR | THE PERSONAL EXPERIENCE'. 192-226: text.
[227]: recent photograph of author. 228-239: *'LAURA (RIDING)
JACKSON: A CHECK-LIST'*. [240]: blank. [241]: Advertisements
for *Selected Poems: In Five Sets* and *The Telling*. [242]: Advertisement for *Chelsea*. [243]: Advertisement for distributor
of *Chelsea*. [244]: blank.

Binding: Paper covers. Front serves as title page. Black
printing on white band for name of magazine and light green
background for title and author. Back repeats facsimile of
author's signature, a rule, and 'author's selections'. Spine
printed lengthwise in green on white band: 'CHELSEA 35'.

Paper: White wove paper. No endpapers.

Contents:

Notes: Published as a special issue of *Chelsea*, this volume
gathers much of Riding's miscellaneous writing of the 1970's.
The price of the magazine was $2.50.

A44   HOW A POEM COMES TO BE   1980

[blue swash letters] A POEM [blue leaf ornament] | [left column:
two-paragraph explanation] | *This is number* [written] 123 [prin-
ted] *of 150.* | COPYRIGHT © *1980 Laura (Riding) Jackson* | [right
column:] *Foreword to the Poem* | [paragraph] | [blue] *How A Poem
Comes To Be* | *For* JAMES F. MATHIAS | [poem of 45 lines, first
three words of first line in blue, rest in black] | LAURA
(RIDING) JACKSON | [signed] Laura (Riding) Jackson

Collation: 22 x 15 in., broadsheet.

Binding: None.

Paper: White Arches wove paper, top and bottom edges untrimmed.

Notes: 150 copies signed by the author were offered by Lord
John Press through Euclid Books at $40.00. The poet's ex-
planation describes this as her first new poem since 1938.

A45   DESCRIPTION OF LIFE   1980

Laura Riding | [red rule] | Description of | Life | Targ
Editions | [red rule] | 1980

Collation: 9 1/4 x 5 3/4 in., unsigned, pp. [i-ii] iii-v [vi]
[1-4] 5-24 [25-26] 27-57 [58-60] 61-75 [76]. [i]: title page.
[ii]: 'Copyright © 1980 Laura (Riding) Jackson | Printed in
the United States of America | All rights reserved'. iii-v:
Preface. [vi]: blank. [1]: 'Description of Life | [rule] |
(from a manuscript of the early 'thirties, | picturing, in
three portraits, the inconclusiveness | of human life | on its
journey to its journey | to its conclusive condition, and
shape)'. [2]: blank. [3]: 'ONE'. [4]: blank. 5-24: text.
[25]: 'TWO'. [26]: blank. 27-57: text. [58]: blank. [59]:
'THREE'. [60]: blank. 61-75: text. [76]: blank. [recto of
back endpaper]: '*Description of Life* by Laura Riding is
Number Eight | of the TARG EDITIONS published in New York
City, on | June 27, 1980. The book was designed by Ronald |
Gordon at The Oliphant Press, New York, and | was printed by
Westbrook. The type is | Baskerville and the paper, Artlaid. |
This first edition is limited | to 350 copies, signed by |
the author. | [signed] Laura (Riding) Jackson'. [verso of
endpaper]: blank.

Binding: Light blue paper over boards. Front and back blank.
Beige cloth on spine extends 3/4 in. onto front and back.
Spine printed in gold: 'Description of Life   Laura Riding'.
All edges trimmed.

Paper: White Artlaid paper. Same endpapers.

Note: Offered for sale by the publisher at $60.00 before pub-
lication and $75.00 thereafter.

B. POEMS IN PERIODICALS
AND BOOKS
(Listed Chronologically)

B1   "Dimensions." *The Fugitive*, 2 (August–September, 1923),
     124.

B2   "A Pair." *Nomad*, 2 (Autumn, 1923), 9.

B3   "Daniel." *The Fugitive*, 2 (October, 1923), 154.

B4   "Adjustment." *The Lyric West*, 3 (November, 1923), 5.

B5   "The Lightning." *The Step Ladder*, 8 (December, 1923), 3.

B6   "The City of Cold Women." *Poetry*, 23 (January, 1924),
     188–190.

B7   "To an Unborn Child." *The Fugitive*, 3 (February, 1924), 9.

B8   "The Quids." *The Fugitive*, 3 (February, 1924), 10–11.

B9   "Initiation." *The Fugitive*, 3 (February, 1924), 12–13.

B10 "Starved." *The Fugitive*, 3 (February, 1924), 14.

B11 "Fallacies." *Poet Lore*, 35 (Spring, 1924), 153–156.

B12 "Improprieties." *The Fugitive*, 3 (April, 1924), 56–57.

B13 "For One Who Will Dust a Shadow." *The Fugitive*, 3 (April,
     1924), 58.

B14 "The Floorwalker." *Contemporary Verse*, 17 (June, 1924),
     91.

B15 "To the Sky." *Contemporary Verse*, 17 (June, 1924), 92.

B16 "For One Who Will Bless the Devil." *The Fugitive*, 3
     (August, 1924), 124.

B17   "Across a Hedge." *Sewanee Review*, 32 (October, 1924), 1.

B18   "Mortal." *The Fugitive*, 3 (December, 1924), 143.

B19   "Forms." *The Fugitive*, 3 (December, 1924), 143.

B20   "Saturday Night." *The Fugitive*, 3 (December, 1924), 144–145.

B21   "Lying Spying." *The Fugitive*, 3 (December, 1924), 146–147.

B22   "Wanderer." *Sewanee Review*, 33 (January, 1925), 56.

B23   "To a Broken Statue." *The Lyric*, 5 (February, 1925), 4.

B24   "For One Who Will Remember." *The Lyric*, 5 (March, 1925), 2.

B25   "Summary for Alastor." *The Fugitive*, 4 (March, 1925), 7.

B26   "The Sad Boy." *The Fugitive*, 4 (March, 1925), 8–9.

B27   "The Higher Order." *The Fugitive*, 4 (March, 1925), 10.

B28   "Druida." *The Fugitive*, 4 (June, 1925), 50–51.

B29   "The Circus." *The Fugitive*, 4 (June, 1925), 52–53.

B30   "Ahead and Around." *The Guardian*, 2 (August, 1925), 377.

B31   "Mary Carey." *The Fugitive*, 4 (September, 1925), 71–72.

B32   "The Only Daughter." *The Fugitive*, 4 (September, 1925), 73.

B33   "Virgin of the Hills." *The Fugitive*, 4 (September, 1925), 74.

B34   "As Well As Any Other." *The Calendar of Modern Letters*, 2 (October, 1925), 91.

B35   "The Higher Order." *The Calendar of Modern Letters*, 2 (October, 1925), 91–92.

B36   "The Contraband." *The Calendar of Modern Letters*, 2 (October, 1925), 92–93.

B37 "Organs of Sense." *The Calendar of Modern Letters*, 2 (October, 1925), 94–100.

B38 "Ode to Love." *The Reviewer*, 5 (October, 1925), 17–19.

B39 "Body's Head." *Poetry*, 27 (November, 1925), 59–66.

B40 "Many Gentlemen." *The Nation*, 18 November 1925, p. 578.

B41 "Sonnets in Memory of Samuel." *The Fugitive*, 4 (December, 1925), 104–108.

B42 "The Fourth Wall." *The Fugitive*, 4 (December, 1925), 109.

B43 "Free." *The Nation*, 27 January 1926, p. 89.

B44 "For One Who Will Sing." *Palms*, 3 (March, 1926), 179.

B45 "For One Who Will Believe." *The Nation*, 11 August 1926, p. 130.

B46 "For All Our Sakes." *The Nation*, 11 August 1926, p. 130.

B47 "How I Called the Ant Darling." *Two Worlds*, 2 (December, 1926), 114. [Name misspelled, "Laura Rider Gottschalk."]

B48 "Sea-Ghost." *transition*, 3 (June, 1927), 113.

B49 "If This Reminds." *transition*, 3 (June, 1927), 114.

B50 "Death as Death." *transition*, 3 (June, 1927), 115.

B51 "The Map of Places." *The Nation*, 15 June 1927, p. 671.

B52 "Love as a Love." *transition*, 6 (September, 1927), 120–124.

B53 "And This Is Loveliness." *transition*, 9 (December, 1927), 138.

B54 "Though in One Time." *transition*, 9 (December, 1927), 139.

B55 "Footfalling." *transition*, 9 (December, 1927), 140.

B56 "One Reason." *The Nation*, 18 January 1928, p. 70.

B57 "Ding-Donging." *transition*, 13 (Summer, 1928), 105.

B58 "All Nothing, Nothing." *transition*, 13 (Summer, 1928), 106–108.

B59   "Sincere Conversations." *The Nation*, 29 August 1928, p. 204.

B60   "Fine Fellow Son of a Poor Fellow." *The Enemy*, 3 (January, 1929), 88-89.

B61   "What Is There to Believe In." *Blues*, 2 (Fall, 1930), 34.

B62   "Preface to These Poems." James Reeves. *The Natural Need*. Deya, Majorca: The Seizin Press and London: Constable, 1935, pp. 7-8.

B63   "A Letter to Any Friend." *Epilogue*, I (Autumn, 1935), 220-221.

B64   "Be Grave, Woman." *Epilogue*, I (Autumn, 1935), 221-222.

B65   "The Need to Confide." *Epilogue*, I (Autumn, 1935), 222-224.

B66   "The Reasons of Each." *Epilogue*, I (Autumn, 1935), 224-226.

B67   "Divestment of Beauty." *Epilogue*, I (Autumn, 1935), 226-227.

B68   "Majorcan Letter, 1935." [With Robert Graves.] *Focus*, IV (December, 1935), 1-9.

B69   "Christmas." *Focus*, IV (December, 1935), 26.

B70   "On a New Generation." *Epilogue*, II (Summer, 1936), 250.

B71   "Because of Clothes." *Epilogue*, II (Summer, 1936), 250-251.

B72   "The Wages of Eloquence." *Epilogue*, II (Summer, 1936), 251-252.

B73   "I Remember." *Epilogue*, III (Spring, 1937), 140-141.

B74   "The Forgiven Past." *Epilogue*, III (Spring, 1937), 141-142.

B75   "The Cycle of Industry." *Epilogue*, III (Spring, 1937), 142-143.

B76   "When Love Becomes Words." *Epilogue*, III (Spring, 1937), 143-148.

B77 "Pride of Head." *Chelsea*, 12 (September, 1962), 11.

B78 "The Definition of Love." *Chelsea*, 12 (September, 1962), 12.

B79 "The Map of Places." *Chelsea*, 12 (September, 1962), 13.

B80 "The Wind Suffers." *Chelsea*, 12 (September, 1962), 14.

B81 "World's End." *Chelsea*, 12 (September, 1962), 15.

B82 "Faith Upon the Waters." *Chelsea*, 12 (September, 1962), 16.

B83 "Advertisement." *Chelsea*, 12 (September, 1962), 17-18.

B84 "Beyond." *Chelsea*, 12 (September, 1962), 18.

B85 "With the Face." *Chelsea*, 12 (September, 1962), 19.

B86 "The Wind, the Clock, the We." *Chelsea*, 12 (September, 1962), 20-21.

B87 "Respect for the Dead." *Chelsea*, 12 (September, 1962), 22-23.

B88 "The World and I." *Chelsea*, 12 (September, 1962), 24.

B89 "On a New Generation." *Chelsea*, 12 (September, 1962), 25.

B90 "I Remember." *Chelsea*, 12 (September, 1962), 26-27.

B91 "Earth." *L'Éphémère*, 11 (1969), 378. With French translation by Anne de Staël and André du Bouchet.

B92 "All Things." *L'Éphémère*, 11 (1969), 382. With French translation by Anne de Staël and André du Bouchet.

B93 "Unless Infinity Is Only Time." *L'Éphémère*, 11 (1969), 386. With French translation by Anne de Staël and André du Bouchet.

B94 "And I." *L'Éphémère*, 11 (1969), 388. With French translation by Anne de Staël and André du Bouchet.

B95 "The World and I." *L'Éphémère*, 11 (1969), 392. With French translation by Anne de Staël and André du Bouchet.

B96   "There Are As Many Questions As Answers." *L'Éphémère*,
        11 (1969), 394. With French translation by Anne de
        Staël and André du Bouchet.

B97   "Poet: A Lying Word." *L'Éphémère*, 11 (1969), 398. With
        French translation by Anne de Staël and André du
        Bouchet.

B98   "The Judgement." *Poetry Pilot*, Academy of American
        Poets, September, 1970, p. 5.

B99   "The Map of Places." *Juillard*, 11 (Winter, 1970-71),
        unpaged.

B100   "From *Voltaire*." *Denver Quarterly*, 8 (Winter, 1974), 35.

B101   "Pride of Head." *Denver Quarterly*, 8 (Winter, 1974), 36.

B102   "Postponement of Self." *Denver Quarterly*, 8 (Winter,
        1974), 37.

B103   "By Crude Rotation." *Denver Quarterly*, 8 (Winter, 1974),
        38-39.

B104   "Jewels and After." *Denver Quarterly*, 8 (Winter, 1974),
        39.

B105   "With the Face." *Denver Quarterly*, 8 (Winter, 1974), 40.

B106   "Unread Pages." *Denver Quarterly*, 8 (Winter, 1974), 41-
        42.

B107   "Fragment." *Denver Quarterly*, 8 (Winter, 1974), 42.

B108   "Auspice of Jewels." *Denver Quarterly*, 8 (Winter, 1974),
        43-45.

B109   "From 'Sickness and Schooling.'" *Denver Quarterly*, 8
        (Winter, 1974), 45.

B110   "After So Much Loss." *Denver Quarterly*, 8 (Winter,
        1974), 46-47.

B111   "In Due Form." *Ms.*, 2 (February, 1974), 52.

C. PROSE IN PERIODICALS AND BOOKS: STORIES, ESSAYS, LETTERS (Listed Chronologically)

C1 "A Prophecy or a Plea." *The Reviewer*, 5 (April, 1925), 1-7.
Essay on poetry.

C2 "The Anthologist in Our Midst." [With Robert Graves.] *The Calendar*, 4 (April, 1927), 22-36. Rpt. *The Calendar of Modern Letters*. Ed. Edgell Rickword and Douglas Garman. New York: Barnes and Noble, 1966.
Essay.

C3 "The New Barbarism and Gertrude Stein." *transition*, 3 (June, 1927), 153-168.
Part IV of essay "T.E. Hulme, the New Barbarism, and Gertrude Stein" in A5.

C4 "In a Café." *transition*, 7 (October, 1927), 31-33. Rpt. C28.
Story.

C5 "Jamais Plus." *transition*, 7 (October, 1927), 139-156.
Essay condensed from "The Facts in the Case of Monsieur Poe" in A5.

C6 [Letter. With Robert Graves.] *Criterion*, 6 (October, 1927), 357-359.
Reply to review of A1 by John Gould Fletcher (H2). His rejoinder appeared later (H3).

C7 "Fragment." *transition*, 10 (January, 1928), 47-48.
Story begins, "There is a woman in this city who loathes me...."

C8 "A Note on *White Buildings* by Hart Crane." *transition*, 10 (January, 1928), 139-141.
Essay.

C9   "Voltaire." *Times Literary Supplement*, 16 February 1928,
        p. 112.
        Letter replying to H5.

C10   "Hungry to Hear." *transition*, 12 (March, 1928), 62.
        Story.

C11   "Mademoiselle Comet." *transition*, 13 (Summer, 1928), 207–
        208.
        Story.

C12   "A Protest." *Saturday Review of Literature*, 11 August
        1928, p. 47.
        Letter replying to H14, review of A7.

C13   "Romantic Criticism." [With Robert Graves.] *Times Literary
        Supplement*, 3 January 1929, p. 12.
        Letter concerning Humbert Wolfe's *Dialogues and Mono-
            logues*.

C14   "Mr. Graves's Poems." *Times Literary Supplement*, 26
        December 1929, p. 1097.
        Letter replying to review of Graves's *Poems, 1929*, 5
        December 1929, p. 1029.

C15   "Modern Riddles." [With Robert Graves.] *Times Literary
        Supplement*, 26 February 1931, p. 154.
        Letter replying to H42, review of A13 and Graves's
            Ten Poems More.

C16   [Letter.] *Time and Tide*, 9 May 1931, p. 556.
        Objecting to H43, review essay by John Collier.

C17   "A Letter." *Americans Abroad, An Anthology*. Ed. Peter
        Neagoe. The Hague, Holland: Servire Press, 1932, pp.
        326–327.
        Reasons for declining to contribute to expatriate
        anthology.

C18   "The Matter of Communication." *Times Literary Supplement*,
        3 March 1932, p. 155.
        Letter replying to H45, review of A14.

C19   [Answers to "An Enquiry."] *New Verse*, 11 (October, 1934),
        3–5.
        Replies to questionnaire sent to forty poets.

C20   "On Reviewing 'Difficult' Books." *Times Literary Supple-
        ment*, 7 March 1936, p. 204.
        Letter replying to H53, review of A29.

C21 "Søren Kierkegaard." *Times Literary Supplement*, 10 April
1937, p. 275.
Letter.

C22 "Riding on Butler." *Time*, 26 April 1937, pp. 4, 6.
Letter defending the integrity of Samuel Butler.

C23 "Neglect of Poets." [With Robert Graves.] *Daily Tele-
graph*, 27 May 1937, p. 16.
Letter.

C24 "Ink of Poppies." *Spectator*, 18 June 1937, p. 1148.
Reply to Dorothy L. Sayers's "Ink of Poppies,"
Spectator, 14 May 1937, pp. 897-898.

C25 "Sour Puss." *New Verse*, n.s. 1 (January, 1939), 30.
Letter replying to H66, review of A35.

C26 "Our 'Modern' Poetry." [With Robert Graves.] *Sunday
Times* (London), 19 February 1939, p. 16.
Letter.

C27 "The Latest in Synonymy." [Schuyler and Laura Jackson.]
Wilson Library Bulletin, 17 (November, 1942), 219, 225.
Essay reviewing *Webster's Dictionary of Synonyms*.

C28 "In a Café." *Transition Workshop*. Ed. Eugene Jolas.
New York: Vanguard Press, 1949, pp. 114-115.
Story.

C29 "Introduction for a Broadcast." *Chelsea*, 12 (September,
1962), 3-5. [BBC Third Programme, April 1, 1962.]
Essay introducing a reading of a selection from A35.

C30 "Continued for *Chelsea*." *Chelsea*, 12 (September, 1962),
6-9.
Essay on poetry expanding C29.

C31 "Presenza della donna nella civiltà attuale." "On the
Role of Women in Contemporary Society." *Civiltà delle
Macchine*, 11 (July-August, 1963), 22-25.
Essay responding to inquiry published in English and
Italian. Rpt. C33.

C32 "Further on Poetry." *Chelsea*, 14 (January, 1964), 38-47.
Essay excerpted from unpublished essay "Poetry and the
Good."

C33 "The Sex Factor in Social Progress." *Chelsea*, 16 (March,
1965), 115-122.
Essay.

C34 "A Last Lesson in Geography." *Art and Literature*, 6
     (Autumn, 1965), 28–43.
     Story from A29 rpt. with sequel author wrote in 1964.

C35 "A Letter to the Editor." *Minnesota Review*, 7 (1967),
     77–79.
     Letter objecting to Michael Kirkham's "The 'Poetic
     Liberation' of Robert Graves," *Minnesota Review*, 6
     (1966), 244–254.

C36 "Correspondence." *Shenandoah*, 18 (Spring, 1967), 67–70.
     Letter objecting to Daniel Hoffman's "Significant
     Wounds: The Early Poetry of Robert Graves," *Shenandoah*,
     17 (Spring, 1966), 21–40.

C37 "Preface for *Chelsea*." *Chelsea*, 20/21 (May, 1967), 114–
     116.
     Essay prefacing C38.

C38 "The Telling." *Chelsea*, 20/21 (May, 1967), 117–162.
     Essay forming core of A41.

C39 "Blue Estuaries." *New York Times Book Review*, 24 November
     1968, p. 52.
     Letter concerning review of Louise Bogan's poems, *The
     Blue Estuaries*, 13 October 1968, p. 4.

C40 "Hungry to Hear." *Juillard*, Pinecone Supplement (Winter,
     1968–69), unpaged.
     Story.

C41 "Poetry, Politics and Truth." *The Observer*, 18 October
     1970, p. 14.
     Letter replying to H122, review of A40.

C42 "Letters." *the Review*, 24 (December, 1970), 75–76.
     Letter replying to H118 and H119.

C43 "The Climate of Criticism." *New York Times Book Review*,
     3 January 1971, p. 14.
     Letter.

C44 "Correspondence." *Modern Language Quarterly*, 32 (December,
     1971), 447–448.
     Letter objecting to H112.

C45 "The Fable of the Dice." *The Predicament of Man: An
     Examination of Policies for the Future*. Ed. Maurice

Goldsmith. Frimley, Surrey: Inforlink Ltd for Science
Policy Foundation, 1972, Section 5, p. 12.
Story with commentary by Alan Clark.

C46 "Laura Riding: Response to Critics." *Massachusetts Review*, 13 (Summer, 1972), 519–520.
Letter.

C47 "The Bondage." *Chelsea*, 30/31 (June, 1972), 24–33.
Essay on women.

C48 "A Postscript." *The Private Library*, n.s. 5 (Autumn,
1972), 139–146.
Essay commenting on H131, concerning the Seizin Press.

C49 "Poems and Paraphrases." *Times Literary Supplement*,
3 November 1972, p. 1342.
Letter objecting to review of James Reeves's *Poems and
Paraphrases*, 4 August 1972, p. 910.

C50 "'The Telling.'" *Times Literary Supplement*, 9 March 1973,
p. 268.
Letter replying to H133, review of A40 and A41.

C51 "The Cult of 'Connections.'" *The Private Library*, n.s. 6
(Autumn, 1973), 133–141.
Letter objecting to Graham Rigby's article, "T.E.
Lawrence and the Seizin Press," *The Private Library*,
6 (Spring, 1973), 16–21.

C52 "Some Autobiographical Corrections of Literary History."
Denver Quarterly, 8 (Winter, 1974), 1–33.
Essay.

C53 "Variously, as to Stories." *Antaeus*, 13/14 (Spring/
Summer, 1974), 50–69.
Essay, excerpts from Preface to A29, and story ("Daisy
and Venison").

C54 "What, If Not a Poem, Poems?" *Denver Quarterly*, 9 (Summer,
1974), 1–13.
Essay.

C55 "Comments on Michael Kirkham's Essay." *Chelsea*, 33 (September, 1974), 153–159.
Essay on H141 in same issue.

C56   "On Ambiguity." *Modern Language Quarterly*, 36 (March,
       1975), 102-106.
       Essay.

C57   "Dr. Gove and the Future of English Dictionaries." *Denver
       Quarterly*, 10 (Spring, 1975), 1-18.
       Essay.

C58   "Supplementary Comment Concerning George Watson's Thinking
       on Noam Chomsky." *Denver Quarterly*, 10 (Spring, 1975),
       19-25.
       Essay.

C59   [Letter.]   *The Nation*, 22 March 1975, p. 322.
       Reply to H145, review of A40.

C60   "Telling." *New York Review of Books*, 2 October 1975,
       pp. 41-42.
       Letter replying to H146, review of A40 and A41.

C61   "Looking Back, Looking Forward." *Stand*, 17 (1976), 40-42.
       Essay.

C62   "Neglected Books." *Antaeus*, 20 (Winter, 1976), 155-157.
       Essay.

C63   "Bertrand Russell, and Others: The Idea of the Master-
       Mind." *Anateus*, 21/22 (Spring/Summer, 1976), 125-135.
       Essay.

C64   "A Private Press." *New York Review of Books*, 29 April
       1976, p. 44.
       Letter objecting to Virgil Thomson's review of Hugh
          Ford's *Published in Paris* (H131), *New York Review of
          Books*, 19 February 1976, pp. 42-44.

C65   "The Fugitives, Etc." *London Magazine*, n.s. 16 (August/
       September, 1976), 90-92.
       Letter objecting to articles by Julian Symons, James
          Atlas, and Kenneth Marshall.

C66   [3 Letters (23 April 1936, 29 April 1936, 15 May 1936).]
       Letters to W.B. Yeats. Ed. Richard Finneran, George
       Mills Harper, and William M. Murphy. Vol. 2. London:
       Macmillan, 1977, pp. 609-611.

C67   "The 'Right English' of Charles M. Doughty." *University
       of Toronto Quarterly*, 46 (Summer, 1977), 309-321.
       Essay.

C68 "Suitable Criticism." *University of Toronto Quarterly*, 47 (Fall, 1977), 74–85.
    Essay reviewing Judith Kroll's *Chapters in a Mythology: The Poetry of Sylvia Plath*.

C69 "Some Notes on Poetry and Poets in This Century, and My Influence." *Poetry Nation Review 9*, 6 (1979), 21–23.
    Essay.

C70 "Laura Riding." *Times Literary Supplement*, 12 September 1980, p. 995.
    Letter replying to H160, review of H158.

C71 [Letter.] *AB Bookman's Weekly*, 1 December 1980, p. 3654.
    Objecting to H165, review of H158.

D. POEMS IN ANTHOLOGIES
(Listed Chronologically)

D1 Braithwaite, William Stanley, ed. *Anthology of Magazine Verse for 1924*. Boston: B.J. Brimmer, 1924, pp. 101-102. ("A Pair")

D2 ————. *Anthology of Magazine Verse for 1925*. Boston: B.J. Brimmer, 1925, pp. 124-127. ("Lying Spying," "The Sad Boy," "Mortal")

D3 Strong, L.A.G., ed. *The Best Poems of 1925*. Boston: Small, Maynard, 1925, pp. 106-107. ("For One Who Will Remember," "Summary for Alastor")

D4 ————. *The Best Poems of 1926*. New York: Dodd, Mead, 1926, pp. 95-96. ("As Well As Any Other," "Many Gentlemen")

D5 ————. *The Best Poems of 1927*. New York: Dodd, Mead, 1928, p. 130. ("For All Our Sakes")

D6 *Fugitives: An Anthology of Verse*. New York: Harcourt, Brace, 1928, pp. 87-100. ("The Poet's Corner," "The Quids," "The Simple Line," "Loss of Reason," "Up a Tree," "Afternoon," "If We Have Heroes," "Death of the Author," "Sunday")

D7 Drinkwater, John, H.S. Canby, and W.R. Benet, eds. *Twentieth Century Poetry*. Boston: Houghton-Mifflin, 1929, pp. 580-582. ("Sea, False Philosophy," "O Vocables of Love")

D8 Roberts, Denys Kilham, Gerald Gould, and John Lehmann, eds. *The Year's Poetry*. London: Bodley Head, 1934, pp. 139-144. ("Midsummer Duet 1934" by Laura Riding & Robert Graves)

D9   Roberts, Michael, ed. *The Faber Book of Modern Verse*.
      London: Faber & Faber, 1936, pp. 211-222. ("The Tilla-
      quils," "Lucrece and Nara," "The Map of Places," "The
      Tiger," "The Wind, the Clock, the We," "The Wind Suffers,"
      "The Flowering Urn," "Nor Is It Written," "Auspice of
      Jewels")

D10   Murphy, Gwendolen, ed. *The Modern Poet*. London: Sidgwick
      & Jackson, 1938, pp. 84-92. Rpt. Miami, Fla.: Granger
      Books, 1976. ("The Quids," "As Many Questions As
      Answers," "Earth," "Doom in Bloom," "The Victory,"
      "After So Much Loss"; Riding is quoted in introduction
      and notes. Alan Clark misidentifies editor as "Rosalie
      Murphy" in A43.)

D11   *A Book of Modern Verse*. London: Chatto & Windus, 1939,
      p. 53. ("As Well As Any Other")

D12   Day Lewis, C., and L.A.G. Strong, eds. *A New Anthology
      of Modern Verse 1920-1940*. London: Methuen, 1941, pp.
      151-152. ("Many Gentlemen," "The Way It Is")

D13   Kreymborg, Alfred, ed. *An Anthology of American Poetry
      1630-1941, Lyric America*. Second Revised Edition.
      New York: Tudor, 1941, pp. 642-643. ("The Wind Suffers")

D14   Ridler, Anne, ed. *The Little Book of Modern Verse*.
      London: Faber & Faber, 1941, pp. 91-92. ("The Tilla-
      quils")

D15   Collins, A.S., ed. *Treasury of Modern Poetry*. London:
      University Tutorial Press, 1947, pp. 165-167. ("Prisms,"
      "So Slight," "Hospitality to Words," "The Wind Suffers")

D16   Williams, Oscar, ed. *A Little Treasury of American
      Poetry*. New York: Scribner's, 1948, pp. 667-677.
      ("The Map of Places," "The Flowering Urn," "Dear Pos-
      sible," "The Wind, the Clock, the We," "Three Sermons
      to the Dead," "For-Ever Morning," "Because of Clothes,"
      "Respect for the Dead," "Auspice of Jewels")

D17   Jolas, Eugene, ed. *Transition Workshop*. New York: Van-
      guard Press, 1949, pp. 254-256. ("All Nothing,
      Nothing")

D18   Ridler, Anne, ed. *The Faber Book of Modern Verse*. Second
      Edition. London: Faber & Faber, 1951, pp. 221-231.
      ("The Tillaquils," "Lucrece and Nara," "The Map of
      Places," "The Tiger," "The Wind Suffers," "The Flowering
      Urn," "Nor Is It Written," "Auspice of Jewels")

**D19 Izzo, Carlo, ed. *Nuovissima Poesia Americana e Negra, 1949-1953*. Parma: Guanda, 1953. ("Respect for the Dead" in English with Italian translation)

**D20 Guterman, N.G., ed. *An Anthology of Modern English and American Verse*. Leningrad: State Publishing House for Education, 1963.

D21 Hall, Donald, ed. *The Faber Book of Modern Verse*. Third Edition. London: Faber & Faber, 1965, pp. 191-197. ("The Tillaquils," "Lucrece and Nara," "The Wind, the Clock, the We," "The Flowering Urn," "Nor Is It Written," "Auspice of Jewels")

D22 Lask, Thomas, ed. *The New York Times Book of Verse*. New York: Macmillan, 1970, pp. 334-335. ("The Troubles of a Book")

D23 Ellmann, Richard, and Robert O'Clair, eds. *The Norton Anthology of Modern Poetry*. New York: W.W. Norton, 1973, pp. 628-633. ("The Map of Places," "Opening of Eyes," "With the Face," "Auspice of Jewels," "Because of Clothes," "The Forgiven Past")

D24 Rothenberg, Jerome, ed. *Revolution of the Word: A New Gathering of American Avant Garde Poetry, 1914-1945*. New York: Seabury Press, 1974, pp. 222-237. ("By Crude Rotation," "Elegy in a Spider's Web," "The Wind, the Clock, the We," "Poet: A Lying Word," from "Memories of Mortalities," "Nothing So Far," prose "Statement of Disagreements")

E. ENTRIES IN REFERENCE BOOKS
(Listed Chronologically)

E1   *Authors Today and Yesterday*. Ed. Stanley J. Kunitz.
      New York: H.W. Wilson Co., 1933, pp. 564-565.
      Autobiographical statement.

E2   *International Who's Who*. 2nd ed. (1937), p. 926.

E3   *International Who's Who*. 3rd ed. (1938), p. 967.

E4   *International Who's Who*. 4th ed. (1939), p. 1024.

E5   *International Who's Who*. 5th ed. (1940), p. 948.

E6   *International Who's Who*. 6th ed. (1941), p. 928.

E7   *International Who's Who*. 7th ed. (1942), p. 784.

E8   *Twentieth Century Authors*. Ed. Stanley J. Kunitz and
      Howard Haycraft. New York: H.W. Wilson Co., 1942,
      p. 1173.
      Autobiographical statement.

E9   *Who's Who* (1942), p. 2633.

E10 *International Who's Who*. 8th ed. (1943-44), p. 721.

E11 *American Authors and Books, 1640-1940*. Ed. W.J. Burke
      and Will D. Howe. New York: Gramercy Publishing Co.,
      1943, p. 631.

E12 *Who's Who* (1943), p. 2629.

E13 *International Who's Who*. 9th ed. (1944-45), p. 732.

E14 *Contemporary American Authors*. Ed. Fred B. Millett.
      New York: Harcourt, Brace and Co., 1944, pp. 542-543.

E15 *Who's Who* (1944), pp. 2324-2325.

E16 *International Who's Who.* 10th ed. (1945-46), p. 739.

E17 *Sixty American Poets, 1896-1944.* Ed. Allen Tate.
     Washington, D.C.: Library of Congress, 1945, pp. 128-
     131.

E18 *Who's Who* (1945), p. 2310.

E19 *Who's Who* (1946), p. 2310.

E20 *International Who's Who.* 11th ed. (1947), p. 742.

E21 *Who's Who* (1947), p. 2331.

E22 *International Who's Who.* 12th ed. (1948), p. 795.

E23 *Who's Who* (1948), p. 2341.

E24 *International Who's Who.* 13th ed. (1949), p. 775.

E25 *Who's Who* (1949), p. 2349.

E26 *International Who's Who.* 14th ed. (1950), p. 789.

E27 *Who's Who* (1950), p. 2362.

E28 *International Who's Who.* 15th ed. (1951), p. 818.

E29 *Who's Who* (1951), p. 2406.

E30 *International Who's Who.* 16th ed. (1952), p. 826.

E31 *Who's Who* (1952), p. 2424.

E32 *International Who's Who.* 17th ed. (1953), p. 851.

E33 *Who's Who* (1953), p. 2487.

E34 *Articles on American Literature, 1900-1950.* Ed. Lewis
     Leary. Durham, N.C.: Duke University Press, 1954,
     p. 257.

E35 Number deleted.

E36 *International Who's Who.* 18th ed. (1954), p. 816.

E37 *Sixty American Poets, 1896–1944.* Rev. ed. Ed. Allen
Tate. Washington, D.C.: Library of Congress, 1954,
pp. 104–106.

E38 *Who's Who* (1954), p. 2478.

E39 *International Who's Who.* 19th ed. (1955), p. 825.

E40 *Twentieth Century Authors, First Supplement.* Ed. Stanley
J. Kunitz. New York: H.W. Wilson, 1955, pp. 482–483.
Autobiographical statement.

E41 *Who's Who* (1955), p. 2499.

E42 *International Who's Who.* 20th ed. (1956), p. 789.

E43 *Who's Who* (1956), p. 2514.

E44 *International Who's Who.* 21st ed. (1957), p. 793.

E45 *Who's Who* (1957), pp. 2551–2552.

E46 *Everyman's Dictionary of Literary Biography, English and
American.* Ed. D.C. Browning. London: J.M. Dent, and
New York: E.P. Dutton, 1958, p. 559.

E47 *International Who's Who.* 22nd ed. (1958), p. 789.

E48 *Who's Who* (1958), p. 2556.

E49 *International Who's Who.* 23rd ed. (1959), p. 747.

E50 *Who's Who* (1959), p. 2571.

E51 *Everyman's Dictionary of Literary Biography, English and
American.* Ed. D.C. Browning. London: J.M. Dent, and
New York: E.P. Dutton, 1960, p. 573.

E52 *International Who's Who.* 24th ed. (1960), p. 795.

E53 *Who's Who* (1960), pp. 2551–2552.

E54 *International Who's Who.* 25th ed. (1961–62), p. 817.

E55 *Who's Who* (1961), p. 2572.

E56 *International Who's Who.* 26th ed. (1962–63), p. 835.

E57 *American Authors and Books, 1640 to the Present Day.* Ed. W.J. Burke and Will D. Howe. Rev. Irving R. Weiss. New York: Crown Publishers, Inc., 1962, p. 617.

E58 *Everyman's Dictionary of Literary Biography, English and American.* Ed. D.C. Browning. London: J.M. Dent, and New York: E.P. Dutton, 1962, p. 573.

E59 *The Reader's Encyclopedia of American Literature.* Ed. Max J. Herzberg. New York: Crowell, 1962, p. 957.

E60 *Who's Who* (1962), p. 2586.

E61 *International Who's Who.* 27th ed. (1963-64), p. 890.

E62 *Concise Encyclopedia of English and American Poets and Poetry.* Ed. Stephen Spender and Donald Hall. New York: Hawthorn Books Inc., 1963, p. 275.

E63 *Who's Who* (1963), pp. 2577-2578.

E64 *International Who's Who.* 28th ed. (1964-65), p. 912.

E65 *Who's Who* (1964), p. 2574.

E66 *International Who's Who.* 29th ed. (1965-66), p. 953.

E67 *Contemporary Authors.* Ed. James M. Ethridge and Barbara Kopala. Vols. 13-14. Detroit, Mich.: Gale Research Co., 1965, p. 229.
     Autobiographical statement.

E68 *Everyman's Dictionary of Literary Biography, English and American.* Ed. D.C. Browning. London: J.M. Dent, and New York: E.P. Dutton, 1965, p. 573.

E69 *Who's Who* (1965), pp. 2587-2588.

E70 *International Who's Who.* 30th ed. (1966-67), p. 1024.

E71 *Who's Who* (1966), p. 2586.

E72 *International Who's Who.* 31st ed. (1967-68), p. 1093.

E73 *Who's Who* (1967), p. 2582.

E74 *International Who's Who.* 32nd ed. (1968-69), p. 1111.

E75 *Who's Who* (1968), pp. 2584-2585.

E76 *International Who's Who.* 32nd ed. (1969-70), p. 1252.

E77 *Everyman's Dictionary of Literary Biography, English and American.* Ed. D.C. Browning. London: J.M. Dent, and New York: E.P. Dutton, 1969, p. 573.

E78 *Who's Who* (1969), p. 2607.

E79 *International Who's Who.* 34th ed. (1970-71), pp. 1345-1346.

E80 *Concise Encyclopedia of English and American Poets and Poetry.* Ed. Stephen Spender and Donald Hall. London: Hutchinson, 1970, pp. 255-256.

E81 *Contemporary Poets of the English Language.* Ed. Rosalie Murphy. New York: St. Martin's Press, 1970, pp. 921-924. Autobiographical statement.

E82 *Who's Who* (1970), p. 2625.

E83 *The Writer's Directory 1971-73.* Ed. A.G. Seaton. New York: St. Martin's Press, 1971, p. 369.

E84 *The Blue Book* (1971-72), pp. 1072-1073.

E85 *International Who's Who.* 35th ed. (1971-72), p. 1377.

E86 *Who's Who* (1971), p. 2659.

E87 *International Who's Who.* 36th ed. (1972-73), pp. 1404-1405.

E88 *American Authors and Books.* Ed. W.J. Burke and Will D. Howe. 3rd rev. ed. New York: Crown Publishers, Inc., 1972, p. 536.

E89 *Who's Who* (1972), p. 2697.

E90 *The Blue Book* (1973-74), p. 1194.

E91 *International Who's Who.* 37th ed. (1973-74), p. 1420.

E92 *Who's Who* (1973), p. 2730.

E93 *The Writer's Directory 1974-76.* London: St. James Press, and New York: St. Martin's Press, 1973, p. 677.

E94 *International Who's Who.* 38th ed. (1974-75), pp. 1455-1456.

E95   *Who's Who* (1974), p. 2765.

E96   *International Who's Who.* 39th ed. (1975-76), p. 1469.

E97   *The Blue Book* (1975), p. 1233.

E98   *Contemporary Literary Criticism.* Ed. Carolyn Riley.
      Vol. 3. Detroit, Mich.: Gale Research Co., 1975,
      pp. 431-432.

E99   *Contemporary Poets.* Ed. James Vinson. 2nd ed. London:
      St. James Press, and New York: St. Martin's Press,
      1975, pp. 1278-1284.
      Autobiographical statement.

E100 *Who's Who* (1975), p. 2664.

E101 *The Writer's Directory 1976-78.* Ed. Nancy E. Duin.
      London: St. James Press, and New York: St. Martin's
      Press, 1976, p. 896.

E102 *International Who's Who.* 40th ed. (1976-77), pp. 1443-
      1444.

E103 *Who's Who in America* (1976-77), p. 1572.

E104 *The Blue Book* (1976), p. 1383.

E105 *Who's Who* (1976), p. 2008.

E106 *International Who's Who.* 41st ed. (1977-78), p. 1449.

E107 *Contemporary Authors.* Ed. Jane A. Bowden. Vols. 65-68.
      Detroit, Mich.: Gale Research Co., 1977, pp. 314-315.
      Autobiographical statement.

E108 *Contemporary Literary Criticism.* Ed. Phillis Carmel
      Mendelson and Dedria Bryfonski. Vol. 7. Detroit,
      Mich.: Gale Research Co., 1977, pp. 373-377.

E109 *Who's Who* (1977), p. 2038.

E110 *International Who's Who.* 42nd ed. (1978-79), pp. 1445-
      1446.

E111 *Who's Who in America* (1978-79), p. 1627.

E112 *Who's Who* (1978), pp. 2070-2071.

E113 *Who's Who* (1979), p. 2116.

F. COLLECTIONS OF MANUSCRIPTS
AND LETTERS
(Listed by Library)

F1 Amherst College: 3 letters.

F2 Boston University: 1 letter.

F3 British Broadcasting Company: Preface to *Four Unposted Letters to Catherine*, appended to BBC script for radio broadcast 15 and 16 July 1963.

F4 Columbia University: Random House Papers, Isidore Schneider Papers, 41 letters.

F5 Cornell University: 21 manuscripts, 94 letters (including letters to James Reeves, Wyndham Lewis), 2 letters to Riding, 1 document, Laura and Schuyler B. Jackson Collection.

F6 Harvard University: Letters to Donald C. MacDonald, Sr., 1959.

F7 Joint University Libraries, Nashville, Tenn.: 7 manuscripts, 46 letters (including letters to Donald Davidson).

F8 Library of Congress (Manuscript Division): 4 letters.

F9 New York Public Library, Berg Collection: 59 letters, 7 documents.

F10 Northwestern University: 7 manuscripts, 25 letters, galleys and page proofs.

F11 Southern Illinois University, Carbondale: 1 manuscript, 12 letters, 5 letters to Riding, 1 memorabilia.

F12 State University of New York at Buffalo: 52 letters (including letters to Alan Hodge), 4 manuscripts.

F13   University of California at Berkeley, Bancroft Library:
        Ralph Withington Church, Robert Edward Duncan Collec-
        tions, 2 letters.

F14   University of Chicago: *Poetry* Collection including
        letters from Riding to Harriet Monroe.

F15   University of Kansas, Lawrence: Letters to J.B. Pinker.

F16   University of Maryland: 82 letters, 1 document.

F17   University of Texas, Austin: 1 manuscript, 64 letters,
        5 letters to Riding, 2 documents.

F18   University of Virginia, Charlottesville: Alida Monroe,
        1 manuscript, 2 letters, 2 letters to Riding.

F19   Yale University, Beinecke Library: 2 manuscripts, 56
        letters (including letters to Gertrude Stein), 6 let-
        ters to Riding, 10 documents.

G. BROADCASTS AND RECORDINGS
(Listed Chronologically)

G1 BBC Third Programme, 1 April 1962. Selection from *Collected
    Poems* (A35) introduced by essay explaining renunciation
    of poetry (C29).

G2 BBC Third Programme, 15 July 1963. Preface and Postscript
    written for broadcast of Letters 1 and 2 of *Four Unposted
    Letters to Catherine* (A10) read by Charlotte Holland.

G3 BBC Third Programme, 16 July 1963. Letters 3 and 4 of
    Four Unposted Letters to Catherine (A10) read by
    Charlotte Holland.

G4 Recording in the Poetry Room of the Harvard College Library.
    Selections from her work with commentary, read by the
    poet for the Poetry Room Collection on 18 January 1972.
    2 reels. WTTB Radio, Vero Beach, Florida. Selection
    includes excerpts from the Preface to *Selected Poems:
    In Five Sets* (A40), *The Telling* (A41), and *Collected
    Poems* (A35). The poems are "The Mask," "The Lullaby,"
    "Death as Death," "The Troubles of a Book," "O Vocables
    of Love," "Earth," "Auspice of Jewels," "Eventual Love,"
    "Nothing So Far," "Doom in Bloom," "Decline of Prophecy,"
    and "The Quids."

H. WRITINGS ABOUT LAURA RIDING
(Listed Chronologically)

H1   Tate, Allen. "Metaphysical Acrobatics." *The New Republic*,
     9 March 1927, p. 76.

     Reviewing *The Close Chaplet*, the first book published by
     Laura Riding Gottschalk, Tate admires the emotional revela-
     tions, wit, irony, mystical vision, and metaphysical in-
     sights but regrets the absence of supporting structure in
     most of the poems. He thinks "The Quids" is the most suc-
     cessful in fusing the data of sensibility and thought.
     This poem characterizes a modern turn to the vocabulary,
     rhetoric, and intent of Elizabethan metaphysical poetry;
     in both periods poetry attempted to portray all kinds of
     experience. In the same review, Tate can also say, "Miss
     Gottschalk, even Miss Gottschalk, performs those emotional
     revelations which give poetry by women much of its charm,
     if not its value...." He predicts she will be a brilliant
     success, since her failures of form are less significant
     than the "power" of her material.

H2   Fletcher, John Gould. [Review of *The Close Chaplet*.] *The
     Criterion*, 6 (August, 1927), 170.

     Failing to see originality in Riding's work, Fletcher
     finds little to admire: "The practiced reader can readily
     distinguish the derivation of her manner: her poems of
     detached and exhaustive comment ... owe nearly everything
     to Miss Marianne Moore; her more serious poems ... come
     from Mr Ransom or Mr Graves; and her more lyrical outbursts
     recall just as persistently Miss Gertrude Stein." His
     favorite poem is "The Lady of the Apple," a plea for the
     female sex.

H3   ————. [Letter.] *The Criterion*, 6 (December, 1927),
     546-547.

     Fletcher replies to Riding's objections (C6) to his
     review of *The Close Chaplet* (H2).

H4   Shanks, Edward. "Modernist Poetry." *Saturday Review of
     Literature*, 10 December 1927, pp. 822-823.

     Review of *A Survey of Modernist Poetry*.

H5   "Modernist Poetry." *Times Literary Supplement*, 19 January
     1928, p. 40.

     This review summarizes *A Survey of Modernist Poetry* and
     arrives at a balanced judgment: "The plain reader is, on
     the whole, treated fairly throughout the book, and in
     gratitude he must persevere in his search for enlightenment
     through a good deal of what may seem to him to be nonsense
     and waste of time."

H6   [Review of *Voltaire*.]   *Times Literary Supplement*, 26
     January 1928, p. 66.

     This negative review ends with a French phrase that
     spurred Riding's rejoinder (C9): "... it is difficult
     indeed to dignify this trivial *jeu d'ésprit* with the title
     of poem."

H7   "The Jungle of Modern Poetry." *Nation and Athenaeum*,
     28 January 1928, p. 654.

     A negative review of *A Survey of Modernist Poetry*.

H8   Bennett, Arnold. "The 'Monstrous Conceit' of Some
     Modernists." *The Evening Standard*, 1 March 1928.
     Rpt. in *Arnold Bennett: The Evening Standard Years,
     "Books and Persons" 1926-1931*. London: Chatto and
     Windus, 1974, pp. 131-133.

     Wittily attacking Riding's *Contemporaries and Snobs*,
     Bennett considers the author intelligent but suffering
     from serious defects: "Miss Riding possesses intellectual
     power; also some intelligence. Also various defects.
     I shall not attempt to state her theory of modernist
     poetry. In order to do so, I should have to read the
     book again, and I would not read it again for £100."
     Generalizing about Riding, Graves, Gertrude Stein, and
     other modernists, Bennett objects to their conceit: "In
     addition to suffering acutely from a total absence of
     humour, these pioneers suffer from the sense of being all
     alone, and utterly right, in an utterly wrong world of
     letters. They rejoice too richly and too contemptuously
     in their apartness. Which is a roundabout way of saying
     that they are monstrous conceited persons. But their
     worst fault is that they cannot write in a comprehensible

fashion." Thinking of Riding's connection with Graves,
Bennett wonders, "I should love to know what Miss Riding
thinks of the admirable but sadly un-modernist poetry of
her collaborator."

H9   Campbell, Roy. "A Question of Taste." *Nation and
      Athenaeum*, 3 March 1928, pp. 817-818.

      Reviewing *Contemporaries and Snobs*, Campbell detected
an attitude in Riding's work that became an obsession:
"She even makes war on the meaning of words, which are
the very signs of the intellect, and succeeds in de-
priving her own words of most of their significance by
means of a specialized formula of definition. Everything
defined by Miss Riding is either the essence of what it
isn't, or the antithesis of what it is. By means of
this facile and rather vulgar habit of paradox she succeeds in escaping quite easily into the 'unknowable.'"

H10   Wilson, Edmund. "The Tennessee Poets." *New Republic*,
      7 March 1928, pp. 103-104.

      Review of *Fugitives, An Anthology of Verse*.

H11   "Books Abroad." *Living Age*, 15 March 1928, pp. 560-561.

      Review of *A Survey of Modernist Poetry*, reprinted from
the *Manchester Guardian*, sounds a nationalistic note:
"The significant fact is that its [modernist poetry's]
leading practitioners are nearly all Americans; for,
however it may be with music, English poetry is not
going to submit to Americanization for the sake of a
Cummings or a Gertrude Stein."

H12   "Contemporary Poetry." *Times Literary Supplement*, 5 April
      1928, p. 254.

      This review of *Contemporaries and Snobs* summarizes
Riding's argument that poetry of the "Zeitgeist" should
be replaced by poetry as a "humanity," and the poet's
subject should be "the individual, the person, the poet."
The reviewer also notes a problem of tone: "Miss Riding
is a very acute critic of the circumstances of modern
poetry. She is a little breathless, like all those who
look round at contemporary conditions and gather them
together in an attempt to make them intelligible in one
synthesis."

H13   Deutsch, Babette. "Poets and Some Others." *Bookman*, 67
      (June, 1928), 442-443.

      Review of *Fugitives, An Anthology of Verse.*

H14   Shanks, Edward. "Anthologies." *Saturday Review of
      Literature*, 7 July 1928, p. 17.

      Review of *A Pamphlet Against Anthologies* disputes
      method of argumentation: "... when you feel you dislike
      a poem, you may condemn it on the ground that it is de-
      fective in logic or in fact, but if you happen to like
      it these considerations do not apply." Riding responded
      in C12.

H15   ————. "They Cannot All Be Right." *London Mercury*, 18
      (August, 1928), 403-412.

      Review of several books discussing poetry including *A
      Survey of Modernist Poetry* and *A Pamphlet Against An-
      thologies.*

H16   "Against Anthologies." *Times Literary Supplement*, 2
      August 1928, p. 564.

      This review of *A Pamphlet Against Anthologies* approves
      of the book: "We are convinced by reason and persuaded,
      at the same time as we are amused, by ridicule that an-
      thologies have a most harmful effect on the general
      appreciation of poetry; that they tend to produce in the
      minds of their readers a composite and blurred picture
      of all poetry, in which all poems about larks, for
      example, become muddled together."

H17   "Anarchism." *Times Literary Supplement*, 16 August 1928,
      p. 590.

      Annoyed by Riding's tone, this reviewer of *Anarchism Is
      Not Enough* explains: "This is a book to which criticism
      cannot be applied--a view in which nobody would more
      cordially agree than the author, whose fluent and gar-
      rulous self-satisfaction is perhaps the most abiding
      memory that one gets from reading it." Certain passages,
      however, are admired: "In this strain, where an original
      imagination is forcibly applied to keen observation, we
      like Miss Riding best." She regards poetry as "pure
      energy not art."

H18   Gates, Barrington. "Cock Robin." *Nation and Athenaeum*,
      22 September 1928, p. 796.

Reviewing *A Pamphlet Against Anthologies*, Gates praises its authors' achievement: "But they have a remarkable dislike of anthologies, and out of this they have made a clever, malicious, and often outrageously funny book. In their view, a little poetry is a disgusting thing: you must read a poet whole or not at all."

H19 [Review of *Contemporaries and Snobs*.] *Boston Evening Transcript*, 24 October 1928, Part 3, p. 2.

Unfavorable review objects to the prose style: "The kernel of meaning to be garnered after infinite labor out of the labyrinthine wordiness of the author's first essay is an elaborate defence and eulogy of independent originality in verse-writing."

H20 Whipple, Leon. "Poets Americano." *Survey*, 1 November 1928, pp. 168-170.

In a long review article, Whipple briefly mentions *A Survey of Modernist Poetry* as support for his belief: "The poem moves you--or it does not. That is all. Our poets are better than we deserve. What they need is an audience, for this age is deaf and blind to poetry."

H21 Kreymborg, Alfred. *Our Singing Strength, An Outline of American Poetry (1620-1930)*. New York: Coward-McCann, 1929, pp. 564-567.

Kreymborg singles out the poem "The Quids" for particular praise, but his interpretation is questionable.

H22 Ransom, Will. *Private Presses and Their Books*. New York: R.R. Bowker Co., 1929, pp. 181-182, 419.

Writing when the Seizin Press was young, Ransom quotes its prospectus: its intentions were "to print necessary books by various particular people. Our editions are decidedly not addressed to collectors but to those interested in work rather than printing--of a certain quality. That is as far in prophecy as we care at the moment to go. You must take our word for it that our reticence is due to something more than an uncertainty of standards. Quite the contrary."

H23 Taggard, Genevieve. "Cat and Mouse." *New York Herald Tribune Books*, 6 January 1929, p. 13.

In this review of *A Survey of Modernist Poetry* and *Contemporaries and Snobs*, Taggard objects to Riding's

tone in the latter book: "In this book she too often
yields to a desire to bewilder and impress her reader
with herself, rather than with the weight and flash of
her ideas."

H24   Gregory, Horace. "Anthologies' Good Effect on Poetry
      Doubted." *New York Evening Post*, 26 January 1929,
      p. 8M.

      Reviewing *A Pamphlet Against Anthologies*, Gregory
      committed an unforgivable faux pas in his introductory
      phrase: "Man and wife, the Riding-Graves are particularly
      exasperated at the bland virtues of a Sir Arthur Quiller-
      Couch, a J.C. Squire or a Robert Bridges."

H25   Troy, William. "Poetry in Vacuo." *New Republic*, 6 Feb-
      ruary 1929, p. 328.

      Reviewing *Contemporaries and Snobs* and *A Survey of
      Modernist Poetry*, Troy rejects their argument: "The
      esthetic idealism of Miss Riding and Mr. Graves unfor-
      tunately exceeds the actual limitations of the human
      mind."

**H26 [Review of *A Survey of Modernist Poetry*.] *St. Louis
      Library Bulletin*, 27 (March, 1929), 79.

H27   Gorman, Herbert. [Review of *A Survey of Modernist Poetry*
      and *A Pamphlet Against Anthologies*.] *Bookman*, 69
      (March, 1929), 104-105.

      Gorman tries to summarize the premise of the argument
      in both books: "To understand the attitude of Miss Riding
      and Mr. Graves (they are apparently two brains that cere-
      brate as one) one must accept the premise from which they
      work: that modern poetry has evolved into an exceedingly
      specialized activity from what was once a rather broad
      'humanity.'"

H28   Diamant, Gertrude. "The Atmosphere Sometimes Too Rare
      for Critic." *New York Evening Post*, 2 March 1929,
      p. 10M.

      Reviewing *Anarchism Is Not Enough*, Diamant turns its
      title against it: "Miss Riding's book is excellent proof
      of its own title. Her anarchism, certainly, is not
      enough." Yet she appreciates Riding's potential
      strengths: "Miss Riding has the equipment of a major
      critic: violent prejudices, a critical apparatus to
      direct these prejudices and a sharp mind to manipulate
      that apparatus."

H29   "Misanthologists." *New York Herald Tribune Books*, 3 March
      1929, p. 20.

      This review of *A Pamphlet Against Anthologies* objects
      to the tone of the argument: "... this diatribe is some-
      times more violent than convincing."

**H30   Hicks, Granville. [Review of *A Pamphlet Against An-
      thologies*.] *New York World*, 10 March 1929, p. 11m.

H31   [Review of *Anarchism Is Not Enough*.] *Boston Evening
      Transcript*, 23 March 1929, Book Section, p. 3.

      The reviewer perceives Riding's individualism as a
      characteristic of modernism: "If individualism is the
      keynote of modernism, then here is a little volume which
      is the quintessence of modernism, for it is individual
      to the nth power. It is a collection of essay-forms
      abounding in cold and concentrated acid from a personality
      which refuses to be absorbed."

H32   [Review of *Anarchism Is Not Enough*.] *The Nation*, 27
      March 1929, p. 380.

      Review summarizes Riding's position as the advocacy of
      "pure individualism, standing completely outside the
      processes of nature and not to be judged with respect to
      any system of extrinsic values."

H33   Hellman, Geoffrey T. "A Lady in a Pet." *New York Herald
      Tribune Books*, 31 March 1929, p. 21.

      This review of *Anarchism Is Not Enough* objects to
      Riding's tone: "Miss Riding's style is epigrammatic ...,
      often antagonizing and bursting over with assurance, her
      ideas, sincerely anti-social, will be found stimulating
      by those who, when they come to occasional examples of
      a conceit which is not only silly but vulgar, do not, in
      a pet, drop 'Anarchism Is Not Enough' into the nearest
      waste-paper basket."

H34   [Review of *A Pamphlet Against Anthologies*.] *The Nation*,
      17 April 1929, p. 492.

      The reviewer concedes, "It is practically impossible
      not to agree with the acid conclusions of Miss Riding and
      Mr. Graves."

H35   MacLeish, Archibald. [Review of *Anarchism Is Not Enough*.]
      Saturday Review of Literature, 20 April 1929, p. 901.

      MacLeish disapproves of Riding's argument but appreciates

her vigor: "She is, I believe, about as wrong as it is
possible to be. Her analysis accepts, as fundamental and
inescapable factors, every sterile, squeamish, and weary
tendency of our time. Her fine protest and rebellion
turns out in the end to be just another resignation.
But she delivers, on the way to that end, some of the
heaviest strokes the smug literature of our (possibly)
age has ever felt."

H36   [Review of *Love as Love, Death as Death*.]   *Times Literary
       Supplement*, 25 April 1929, p. 343.

       Reviewer finds Riding's faults outweigh her virtues:
       "Elliptic and abstruse, Miss Riding's poems are sometimes
       witty and sometimes appear to be penetrating."

H37   Hutchison, Percy. "The Case For and Against the Poetry
       Anthology." *New York Times Book Review*, 23 June 1929,
       p. ·2.

       Reviewing *A Pamphlet Against Anthologies*, Hutchison
       finds the joke falls flat: "They are only moderately
       funny."

H38   "The New Books." *Saturday Review of Literature*, 17
       August 1929, p. 63.

       This review of *A Pamphlet Against Anthologies* judges
       it "perfectly sound in intention, yet singularly offensive
       in execution."

H39   Kallen, H.M. "Ineffable Snark." *Saturday Review of
       Literature*, 31 August 1929, pp. 85-87.

       In a long review essay on *A Survey of Modernist Poetry*
       and *Contemporaries and Snobs*, Kallen attributes the con-
       tradictions in the arguments of both books to the "dis-
       turbed emotions" of their authors. Interpreting the
       modernist movement as an effort to achieve an identity
       between words as symbols and meaning, he chides it for
       pursuing a chimera: "The modernist spirit has been one
       which strives after this impossibility ... it is hunting
       an ineffable Snark."

H40   [Matthews, T.S. Review of *Anarchism Is Not Enough*.]
       Bookman, 70 (September, 1929), 106.

       Although this review is unsigned, the review of another
       book following it is attributed to Matthews, and he
       quotes this passage expressing his early impressions of

Riding in *Jacks or Better* (H152), p. 139: "To read her book is like listening to a man who is passionately anxious to be heard, but who has such an impediment in his speech that he cannot be understood."

H41 Dodd, Lee Wilson. "No Thoroughfare." *Saturday Review of Literature*, 27 December 1930, p. 486.

Dodd tries to understand the alien poetry of the "metaphysical school" in which he places Hart Crane and Laura Riding. It is not merely the obscurity of Riding's poetry that Dodd dislikes, but he recognizes her effort to "sever herself from the normal emotional contacts with this common world of common men" and considers this endeavor "soliloquy in the absolute sense" of the word. His premises are exactly opposite to hers: "The emotions are shared by us all; it is the higher association centers that separate man from man."

H42 "Modern Riddles." *Times Literary Supplement*, 1 January 1931, p. 8.

This review of *Twenty Poems Less* wryly notes that Riding "cannot help appearing to make some inquiry into the recesses of the mind, and may very well be doing so, though it is hard to say." Robert Graves's *Ten Poems More* is also discussed; Graves and Riding responded to the notice in C15.

H43 Collier, John. "A Modernist." *Time and Tide*, 28 March 1931, pp. 388, 390.

Reviewing *Contemporaries and Snobs*, *Anarchism Is Not Enough*, *Poems: A Joking Word*, and *Experts Are Puzzled*, Collier prefers Riding's essays to her poetry. His article prompted Riding's angry letter to the magazine (C16). Riding's letter, in turn, provoked Virginia Woolf's disparaging remarks to Ethel Smyth (H156).

H44 "A Difficult Writer." *Times Literary Supplement*, 28 May 1931, p. 422.

Reviewing *Poems: A Joking Word*, *Experts Are Puzzled*, *Though Gently*, and *Four Unposted Letters to Catherine*, the reviewer tries to analyze the underlying cause of the difficulty of much of Riding's poetry: "... it is due to her need to state deeply felt personal experience in terms equally personal."

H45   "Laura and Francisca." *Times Literary Supplement*, 11
      February 1932, p. 92.

      Brief notice of *Laura and Francisca* which occasioned
      Riding's reply, C18. Reviewer complained of the difficulty
      of knowing what the poem was trying to communicate.

H46   Wheelwright, John. "Multiplied Bewilderment." *Poetry*,
      40 (August, 1932), 288-290.

      Reviewing *Poems: A Joking Word* and *Laura and Francisca*,
      Wheelwright faults Riding for failing to accomplish her
      goal of articulating thought: "She has contrived fresh
      word phrases; she has, as she says, a whole dictionary
      of un-words; but it is the syntax which she has not mas-
      tered. Most of her poems are too long, and while most
      of them are not clear enough, many, like *The Nightmare*
      with its unnecessary signposts, are too clear. It is
      conscious thought that she has not thought about."

H47   MacNeice, Louis. "Miss Riding's Death." *New Verse*, 6
      (December, 1933), 18-19.

      Reviewing *The Life of the Dead*, MacNeice contrasts it
      favorably with her earlier work: "All her previous
      poetry which I have read has seemed to me appallingly
      bleak and jejune. 'Voltaire' was futile, 'Laura and
      Francisca' dreary, 'A Joking Word' appealed by its blend
      of subtlety and naïveté but most of its tropes were too
      facile (there is nothing so easy as rehashing meta-
      physical paradox)." Recognizing Riding's desire to ex-
      press the truth about death, he contrasts good philosophy
      with good poetry. Riding "lacks a healthy vulgarity and
      Death, I think, is not readable about unless slightly
      vulgarised."

H48   "14A." *Times Literary Supplement*, 1 March 1934, p. 142.

      Brief favorable review praises the story's liveliness.

H49   "Miss Riding's Poems." *Times Literary Supplement*, 3 May
      1934, p. 318.

      This review of *Poet: A Lying Word* and *The Life of the
      Dead* recognizes Riding's interest in "the silent half of
      language" yet concludes: "But we are left wondering,
      noting her skill, what weariness or accident has turned
      her from the objective sensuous world of poetry to explore
      the inarticulate deserts, which she calls death."

H50 [Review of *Americans*.] *New York Herald Tribune Books*,
 3 February 1935, p. 14.

 This brief review of *Americans* concludes: "The writing
 is too often of a stillborn nature: the dice are loaded
 and the hand is shaky."

H51 Benét, William Rose. [Review of *Americans*.] *Saturday
 Review of Literature*, 9 February 1935, p. 479.

 Benét considers the poem "pretty much doggerel."

H52 Roberts, Michael. "Introduction." *The Faber Book of
 Modern Verse*. London: Faber & Faber, 1936, pp. 1-35.

 When Roberts invited Riding and Graves to submit poems
 for his anthology, they replied with a set of conditions,
 including the requirement that they approve the introduction. As a result, his analysis of modern poetry owes
 much to them, especially his characterization of two
 schools of English poetry, one headed by Eliot, the
 other led by Riding and Graves. Roberts calls Eliot's
 "European" and contrasts it with the "view of poetry
 which Laura Riding has increasingly emphasized--poetry
 as the final residue of significance in language, freed
 from extrinsic decoration, superficial contemporaneity,
 and didactic bias."

H53 "Story and Idea." *Times Literary Supplement*, 22 February
 1936, p. 159.

 This review of *Progress of Stories* describes Riding's
 stories as parables whose meanings are not made clear;
 moralizing and metaphysical disquisition overwhelm the
 storytelling. Riding replied to charges of being "difficult" in C20.

H54 Muir, Edwin. "New Novels." *The Listener*, 25 March
 1936, p. 604.

 Muir praises *Progress of Stories* effusively: "Miss
 Riding has enough invention for half-a-dozen novelists,
 and enough intellectual power for a score. She is witty,
 she is a delightful story-teller, and her style at its
 best has the perfect ease which comes from being able to
 say in the simplest words exactly what one wants to say."

**H55 Calder-Marshall, Arthur. [Review of *Progress of Stories*.]
 New Stories, 2 (Autumn, 1936), 638-639.

H56 "A Dream of Troy." *Times Literary Supplement*, 27 March
      1937, p. 239.

      This review of *A Trojan Ending* shrewdly observes, "At
      first sight this seems to be an attempt to do for Troy
      what Mr. Robert Graves has done for the Julio-Claudians....
      Yet the comparison is superficial." The difference is
      that Troy has a strong personal meaning for Riding: "To
      those who know, the book will be a rich dream and a
      delight; of those who come to it without special knowledge
      it may demand more patience than the novelist can claim."

H57 Gibson, Wilfrid. "New Novels." *Manchester Guardian*, 30
      March 1937, p. 5.

      Reviewing *A Trojan Ending*, Gibson contrasts its
      qualities with the faults of Riding's poetry: he read
      the book "with absorbed interest, only regretting that I
      could not take it at a more leisurely pace, thrilled by
      the lucid beauty of Miss Riding's prose, which was in
      the nature of being a pleasant surprise to a reader who
      had too frequently been baffled in his attempts to ex-
      tract some inkling of a meaning from her difficult and
      abstruse verse." He describes Cressida in the novel as
      "an embodiment of her creator's own personality."

H58 MacNeice, Louis. [Review of *A Trojan Ending*.] *Spectator*,
      2 April 1937, p. 632.

      MacNeice admires the style of the writing for its
      "living prose rhythm."

H59 Shawe-Taylor, Desmond. "New Novels." *New Statesman and
      Nation*, 3 April 1937, p. 559.

      Reviewing *A Trojan Ending*, Shawe-Taylor expresses his
      impatience: "It is untiring, pointless, and wildly
      boring...."

H60 Erskine, John. "Laura Riding's New Story of Troy and
      Cressida." *New York Times Book Review*, 15 August 1937,
      p. 6.

      A review of *A Trojan Ending*.

H61 Holliday, Terrence. "A Fresh Story of Old Troy." *New
      York Herald Tribune Books*, 15 August 1937, p. 4.

      This admiring review of *A Trojan Ending* praises Riding
      lavishly: "... she has chosen one of the noblest and most
      splendid themes in Western literature, and this she has

so beautifully developed and skillfully orchestrated as
to challenge comparison on even terms with all but the
greatest of her predecessors."

H62 "Troy." *Time*, 16 August 1937, pp. 63–64.

Favorable review of *A Trojan Ending*.

H63 Davenport, Basil. "Laura Riding and the Heroic Spirit."
Saturday Review of Literature, 11 September 1937, p. 11.

Review of *A Trojan Ending*.

H64 Van Doren, Mark. "Cressida of Troy." *The Nation*, 11
September 1937, p. 271.

Reviewing *A Trojan Ending*, Van Doren sees that for
Riding, "Troy is a symbol of whatever in humanity is
most precious. But it is equally obvious that a reader
who comes to her without an identical symbol will not be
compelled to believe her, and will not even discover
what it is that is so precious." Yet he appreciates the
book's assets: "At its center, therefore, the book is
vague. But its surface is frequently very fine."

H65 Vaughan, Richard. "Truth Lushed to Earth." *New Republic*, 6 October 1937, p. 250.

Review of *Progress of Stories* and *A Trojan Ending*.

H66 [Grigson, Geoffrey.] "First of All, Miss Laura Riding."
New Verse, 31–32 (Autumn, 1938), 24–26.

A hostile review of Riding's *Collected Poems* uses
Riding's favorite word, "dead," as a term of disapproba-
tion. Riding's special use of the word to indicate what
is permanent, eternal, immutable, is lost in the ordinary
use of the word as a synonym for bad. The review betrays
the bitterness of disillusionment: "In fact, Miss Riding
is the Queen-bore among all poets writing at present.
She must face that truth. She was useful to some of us
when we were young, like Brancusi's egg; but there isn't
so much difference between eggs, so why go on being the
Heroine of the Poultry Farm and the champion layer? Miss
Riding's bullying must be refused and her ghostly bluff
must be called." The page facing the review advertises
Riding's *Collected Poems* with complimentary quotations
from Julian Symons, Richard Church, and Stephen Spender.
Riding retorted in C25.

H67 [Smith, Janet Adam. Review of *Collected Poems*.] *The
     Criterion*, 18 (October, 1938), 113-115.

     This review achieves a rare balance between appreciating
     Riding's success in realizing her goals and disagreeing
     with the value of those goals. Smith perceptively
     describes the characteristics of Riding's poems yet
     regrets the absence of sensory description. Riding "seems
     to be trying to make us apprehend universals as vividly as
     we usually apprehend particulars. But if this process is
     carried too far for the reader, he may feel that the poems
     end by losing reference to anything outside the mesh of
     language."

H68 "The Purpose of Poetry." *Times Literary Supplement*, 8
     October 1938, p. 637.

     Put off by the tone of her preface, the reviewer of
     her *Collected Poems* extends his objections to Riding's
     prose to her poetry: "But there is, of course, the
     possibility that they [her poems] are obscure in the
     same fashion as the introduction, and for much the same
     reason, because their profundities are vague, their
     arguments disconnected, their terms often used in a
     private sense."

H69 De Selincourt, Basil. "Difficult Simplicity." *Manchester
     Guardian*, 11 October 1938, p. 7.

     In an admiring review of Riding's *Collected Poems*,
     De Selincourt observes: "Her own idea is to achieve unity
     by negation, by peeling off the trappings, layer by layer
     until the onion is gone. She forgets that the whole
     and the parts are indivisible."

H70 "Light and Leading." *Times Literary Supplement*, 26 Novem-
     ber 1938, p. 751.

     Favorable review of *The World and Ourselves*.

H71 "The World and Ourselves." *Times Literary Supplement*,
     26 November 1938, p. 755.

     Article on the significance of a poet writing a book
     like *The World and Ourselves*.

H72 Porteus, Hugh Gordon. "Reading and Riding." *Twentieth
     Century Verse*, 14 (December, 1938), 130-132.

     Reviewing her *Collected Poems*, Porteus recognizes
     Riding's quest for purity, but he disapproves: "And her

use of words, though not so purely abstract as Gertrude
Stein's, is too nearly and too priggishly pure to arouse
or compel the interest of poor impure readers. All that
is human, including personality and the arts, must be
impure, with a high value attaching to specific im-
purities. 'Pure' art is non-human, unconscious, is nest
or crystal, torpedo or scarab, organic or mechanic. Miss
Riding's poems have all their colours washed out, they
mean well but too much to mean anything with precision,
they bid you a coldly polite good-bye." Worse, he accuses her of fraud: "Her style is shoppy and dressy; it
may be by turns svelte or stark, but always it appears
all the fussier for trying to be unfussy."

H73 Berryman, John. "A Philosophical Poet." *New York Herald
     Tribune Books*, 11 December 1938, p. 21.

     Making an effort to be generous in his review of her
     Collected Poems, Berryman tries to judge Riding by her
     best work rather than her typical, abstract poems. He
     admires "the brilliant, fantastic poems about imaginary
     people" and "the poems written by the poet as a dis-
     tinctly feminine sensibility, which are as remarkable
     for their tact as for their delicacy and directness."

H74 Bogan, Louise. [Review of *Collected Poems*.] *New Yorker*,
     24 December 1938, p. 59.

     Unpleasant, unfavorable, brief notice.

H75 [Jackson, Schuyler B.] "Nine and Two." *Time*, 26 Decem-
     ber 1938, pp. 41-44.

     Although this review of Riding's *Collected Poems* was
     unsigned, Jackson claimed authorship in a note appended
     to the Cornell University Library's collection. He adds
     that T.S. Matthews, then an editor at *Time*, collaborated
     in composing the brief notices on eleven recently pub-
     lished books of poems. The article pays highest tribute
     to Laura Riding, "the most difficult and at the same
     time the most lucid of present-day poets," rating her
     above such rivals as William Carlos Williams, Robinson
     Jeffers, Donald Davidson, and Kay Boyle. Only Riding
     and Rilke rank as writers who "make the word poet make
     sense." Perhaps Matthews, who had met Riding and Graves
     in Majorca, guided Jackson to the terms of praise that
     Riding would find most acceptable: "The main difficulty
     for U.S. readers will probably be that she writes in a
     language in which every word carries its fullest literate
     meaning."

H76   Moore, Merrill. *The Fugitive, Clippings and Comment*.
      Boston: privately printed, 1939.

      Himself a member of the Fugitive Group, Moore collected
      and privately published notices from Nashville news-
      papers and national reviews that provide a contemporary
      record of the development of the group. After Riding
      was invited to become a member, she was named in the
      group's publicity announcements and was cited by re-
      viewers as a full-fledged Fugitive.

H77   Fitts, Dudley. "The 'Right Reasons' for Writing Poetry."
      Saturday Review, 25 March 1939, p. 17.

      Fitts objects to the excessive abstraction in Riding's
      poetry and rebels against the tone of her introduction
      to her *Collected Poems*: "Hauteur is a potent persuasive;
      but it must be confessed that Miss Riding has few equals,
      when it comes to browbeating an audience into conviction
      by sheer force of arrogance, among any poets living or
      dead."

H78   Hays, H.R. "The Expatriate Consciousness." *Poetry*, 54
      (May, 1939), 101-104.

      Recognizing the possibility that Riding may be reacting
      against the typical sentimental poetry of women, Hays
      nevertheless finds her *Collected Poems* too remote from
      actual life: "Miss Riding's technical maturity is not to
      be questioned; there is felicity of phrase and originality
      in abundance, yet the bulk of the work seems to be a
      substitute for life rather than the product of integrated
      experience. There is such a barren rejection of all
      sensuality, (even word-color), such an imprisoning self-
      consciousness, such a dry dissection of the last cerebral
      quiver, that one is driven to psycho-analytical conjecture
      to find excuses for many of the poems."

H79   Fitzgerald, Robert. "Laura Riding." *Kenyon Review*, 1
      (Summer, 1939), 341-345.

      This review of Riding's *Collected Poems* accepts the
      definition of poetry presented in the preface and praises
      the poems accordingly: "The authority, the dignity of
      truth telling, lost by poetry to science may gradually
      be regained. If it is, these poems should one day be a
      kind of *Principia*. They argue that the art of language
      is the most fitting instrument with which to press upon
      full reality and make it known." Her landscape is the

"country of the mind," a cosmology she describes with precision.

H80 "Cells of Authorship, An Attack on Red Literature."
     Times Literary Supplement, 10 June 1939, p. 345.

     Appreciative review of *The Left Heresy in Literature
     and Life* observes that the attack on the left is "infec-
     ted with some of the qualities" the book deplores—
     argumentativeness, contempt, love of generalization, and
     anger.

H81 Pruette, Lorine. "The Women the Men Married." *New York
     Herald Tribune Books*, 3 September 1939, p. 8.

     Disliking *Lives of Wives*, Pruette sympathizes with the
     husbands who were cursed with such "detestable females."

H82 "How Wives of the Conquerors Helped Shape World's His-
     tory." *Newsweek*, 4 September 1939, p. 31.

     Review of *Lives of Wives* concludes, "It fails because
     of a surfeit of material."

H83 [Review of *Lives of Wives*.] *The New Yorker*, 9 September
     1939, p. 78.

     Reviewer observes, "Great men are probably a nuisance
     and their wives more interesting than historians give
     them credit for, but it's hard to prove."

H84 Owens, Olga. "Wives of Heroes." *Boston Evening Transcript*,
     9 September 1939, Part 4, p. 2.

     Favorable review of *Lives of Wives*.

H85 Pratt, Fletcher. "Ancient Ladies." *Saturday Review of
     Literature*, 9 September 1939, p. 16.

     Review of *Lives of Wives*.

H86 "In Man's Image." *Time*, 11 September 1939, pp. 90-91.

     Review of *Lives of Wives*.

H87 West, Anthony. "New Novels." *New Statesman and Nation*,
     16 September 1939, p. 405.

     Review of *Lives of Wives*.

H88   Greene, Graham. [Review of *Lives of Wives*.] *Spectator*,
        22 September 1939, p. 420.

        Greene finds the novel boring and unsuccessful in terms
        of its author's avowed intentions: "... the women are
        soon edged into the outer circle, and we are left in the
        dry company of dates, generals, sieges." Greene perceives
        the source of the book's "unreadability": "Miss Riding is
        so afraid of falsity that her prose has the grapenut
        quality of a school text-book. She picks out her adjec-
        tives like a prim woman removing the bones from a kipper."

H89   Kazin, Alfred. "Wives of Heroes." *New York Times Book
        Review*, 24 September 1939, pp. 6-7.

        Reviewing *Lives of Wives*, Kazin admires it: "It is not
        a book of feminine solidarity; what interests Miss Riding
        is that fascination that steals through all memoirs of
        royalty, the difference between appearance and reality
        that is vividly dramatized in manners."

**H90 [Review of *Lives of Wives*.] *Christian Science Monitor*,
        30 September 1939, p. 10.

H91   "Wives of Great Men." *Times Literary Supplement*, 21 Oc-
        tober 1939, p. 610.

        This review of *Lives of Wives* balances its successes
        against its failures: "Throughout the work, the ancient
        background is brilliant, colourful and scholarly in
        detail, but there are no new lights; and putting the book
        down, one is left with a feeling of flatness. That may
        have been the writer's intention. If that is so, the
        very negativeness of her thesis, that the great men of
        these ages were far less great than their women, has
        robbed her book of its legitimate vitality."

H92   Moult, Thomas. "Short Stories." *Manchester Guardian*,
        24 October 1939, p. 3.

        This brief review of *Lives of Wives* detects the at-
        tribute of the book that continued to interest its author:
        "Miss Riding's considerable gift is shown at its best in
        her historical fiction.... In slow-moving, carefully
        chosen prose--the prose of one who is in her unconven-
        tional, exasperating fashion a true poet--she brings to
        life such fascinating figures as Aristotle, Alexander
        the Great, Herod, and certain women and wives, and also
        their times."

H93   Blackmur, Richard P.   [Review of *Collected Poems*.]
      Partisan Review, 6 (Winter, 1939), 108-115.

      Objecting to Riding's use of negative forms and
      nihilistic views, Blackmur writes: "Miss Riding is the
      not star of un no not never nowhere.... she is jetsam:
      washed up; and just to the level that *we* are washed up
      she makes excellent reading."

H94   Yeats, W.B. *Letters on Poetry from W.B. Yeats to
      Dorothy Wellesley*. London: Oxford University Press,
      1940, pp. 64-69.

      Yeats reports his correspondence with Riding and Graves
      in 1936 concerning their contributions to his edition of
      the *Faber Book of Modern Verse*, which appeared in 1938.
      He refused to comply with her conditions and criticized
      her idea of poetry: "her school was too thoughtful,
      reasonable & truthful, ... poets were good liars who
      never forgot that the Muses were women who liked the
      embrace of gay warty lads."

H95   Gregory, Horace, and Marya Zaturenska. *A History of
      American Poetry, 1900-1940*. New York: Harcourt, Brace
      and World, 1946. Rpt. Gordian Press, 1969.

      An account of the Fugitive Group leads to an assessment
      of Laura Riding; she is admired not as a poet but as a
      "colorful" writer of prose. She served poetry best as
      an "unofficial and unacknowledged emissary of the Nash-
      ville Fugitives in postwar Europe." Her personality is
      conveyed by the report that her bedroom wall in her
      house in Majorca bore the inscription in gold letters:
      "God is a Woman." Disparaging her *Collected Poems* by
      quoting some of the least memorable lines from her
      earliest poem, "The Vain Life of Voltaire," Gregory and
      Zaturenska call her an "industrious, earnest, and ungifted
      amateur." They prefer *A Pamphlet Against Anthologies*
      for its iconoclasm and irreverence.

H96   Ransom, Will. *Selective Check Lists of Press Books*. *Part
      II*. New York: Phillip C. Duschnes, 1946, p. 64.

      Incomplete list of Seizin Press publications.

H97   Raiziss, Sonia. "An Estimate of Laura Riding." *Con-
      temporary Poetry*, 6 (Autumn, 1946), 14-17.

      Comparing Riding to other members of the Fugitive
      Group, Raiziss perceives Elizabethan, symbolist, sophis-

ticated modern and especially metaphysical influences
in all of them. Riding is the most metaphysical of
the group. Her poems seem algebraic in their logic,
abstraction, and economy. "Riding divests feelings of
feeling, and then works with their exact equivalents in
the intense abstract." She is a *"namer,"* who seeks the
"lowest common denominator" of reality by stripping
language to its essence. In place of imagery or rhyme,
she presents "a poetry of syntactical relationships
among notions."

H98   ————. *La Poésie Américaine "Moderniste" 1910-1940.*
       Trans. Charles Cestre. Paris: Mercure de France,
       1948, pp. 53-54.

       A brief description of Riding as an example of American
modernism.

H99   ————. *The Metaphysical Passion. Seven Modern American*
       Poets and the Seventeenth-Century Tradition. Philadel-
       phia: University of Pennsylvania Press, 1952, passim.

       Raiziss offers Riding as an example of the "modern
metaphysical impulse in American literature" (p. 15).
Riding and Graves's chapter in *A Survey of Modernist*
Poetry on "The Humourous Element in Modernist Poetry"
leads Raiziss to a comparison of the modern to the
seventeenth-century poets' twofold use of wit: both
turn irony on themselves and on society. The chief attributes of modernist poetry--including a passionate
self-consciousness, an apparently noncommittal tone,
historical relativism, and experimentation in prosody,
rhetoric, and idiom--are seen as a resurgence of the
seventeenth century's metaphysical spirit.

H100   Southworth, James G. *More Modern American Poets.*
       Oxford: Basil Blackwell, 1954, pp. 103-113.

       In Southworth's judgment, Riding's best poems "deal
with the subject of love, experienced or sublimated, in
which the experiences described are closest to the
realm of actuality. It is in these poems, and those
dealing with the spiritual barrenness that the common
reader will find Miss Riding at her best."

H101   Jarrell, Randall. "Graves and the White Goddess--Part
       II." *Yale Review*, 45 (1956), 467-478.

       In his insightful analysis of the development of
Robert Graves's poetry, Jarrell identifies Riding as

"the White Goddess incarnate, the Mother-Muse in contemporary flesh."

H102   Fuller, Roy. "Some Vintages of Graves." *London Magazine*, 5 (February, 1958), 56-59.

Fuller considers Graves's development as a poet the result of his association with Riding: "One may guess that it was Miss Riding's stern critical standards that finally expunged from his verse not only the remains of the anodynic tradition, but also those extended and sterile satirical versifications, the chummy literary verse letters, the imitations of Skelton, and so forth, that he was still writing up to 1925. The poems of the ensuing period constitute (at the moment) Graves's real achievement...."

H103   Cowan, Louise. *The Fugitive Group, A Literary History*. Baton Rouge: Louisiana State University Press, 1959.

Cowan's account of the publication of the little magazine *The Fugitive* in the early 1920's by a group of poets living in Nashville--including John Crowe Ransom, Donald Davidson, Allen Tate, and Robert Penn Warren-- denigrates Riding's contributions but provides a picture of the other Fugitives' personal reactions to her. While submitting her poems to many little magazines, Laura Riding Gottschalk found her work welcomed most warmly by *The Fugitive*. She won a contest it sponsored, became a regular contributor, and was represented in almost every issue after she joined the group. Cowan continues her history through the publication of *Fugitives: An Anthology of Verse* in 1928 and includes a list of the contents of each issue of the magazine (1922-25).

H104   Matthews, T.S. *Name and Address*. New York: Simon and Schuster, 1960.

This autobiography portrays Schuyler B. Jackson, Riding's second husband, as a brilliant, intense, promising poet. The two men were friends from their days at Princeton until 1939. Matthews felt Jackson was "mad with pride and literally bewitched." Their last association was a series of meetings to write a "Protocol" which "by the sternness of its thought and the authority of its language would arrest the drift of the world into the war we saw coming."

H105   Raiziss, Sonia. "An Appreciation." *Chelsea*, 12 (September, 1962), 28-31.

Influenced by her correspondence with Riding, Raiziss retreats from her earlier description of her poetry as "metaphysical": Riding has a "shrewd and unusual wit-- not quite the expected metaphysical." Her art is "nonobjectivist.... It wants to *name* not describe the occasion, substance, issue, with its intrinsic delicacy or drama.... Feeling is certainly here, but emotion is stripped. And the nakedness is good to look at."

H106   Day, Douglas. *Swifter Than Reason, The Poetry and Criticism of Robert Graves*. Chapel Hill: University of North Carolina Press, 1963.

Intending to write a critical biography of Robert Graves, Day found he had to account for Riding's role in Graves's development. Day compares Riding's poetry unfavorably to Graves's: her poems seem abstract, lifeless, dryly cerebral, coldly theoretical to Day. Their lack of "verbal discipline and rhythmic pattern of any kind, cause one to disbelieve that Miss Riding could have taught Graves, from the earliest days of his career a highly skilled technician, much about prosody." Nevertheless, Day is forced to acknowledge the influence Graves attributes to Riding. She "restored his confidence in himself and his profession, and ... forced him to give his whole concentration to the perfection of his poems." Day interprets allusions to Isis in Graves's "As It Were Poems" as references to Riding's role as a goddess whom he willingly served.

H107   Moran, James. "The Seizin Press of Laura Riding and Robert Graves." *The Black Art*, 2 (Summer, 1963), 35-37.

Moran's account is influenced by Robert Graves's recollections: "Seizin means 'possession' and signified, in the words of Graves, 'that we were our own masters and no longer dependent on publishers who would tell us that our poems did not fit the image of poetry which they wished to present to the public'. They also liked the 'z' in Seizin, it seems." Moran includes Jay Macpherson's *Nine Poems* (Palma, 1955) as a Seizin book, but Riding disputes the use of the Seizin imprint after 1939, when she and Graves parted. She counters Moran's version in a Postscript (C48) to Hugh Ford's "The Seizin Press" (H131).

H108 Turner, Michael. "The Seizin Press—An Additional Note."
The Black Art, 2 (Autumn, 1963), 84-86.

Turner offers additions and corrections to James
Moran's article (H107) and quotes a letter written by
Robert Graves in the late 1920's regarding Riding's
work and their plans for the Seizin Press.

H109 Symons, Julian. "An Evening in Maida Vale." *The London
Magazine*, n.s. 3 (January, 1964), 34-41. Rpt. in
Critical Occasions. London: Hamish Hamilton, 1966,
pp. 206-213. Excerpts quoted in *Contemporary Literary
Criticism*. Ed. Carolyn Riley. Detroit: Gale Research
Co., 1975, pp. 431-432.

A memoir of Symons's meeting with Riding in 1939 expands
to a critical estimate of her and Graves's importance as
non-Leftist writers in the 1930's. He admired Riding's
work and requested a contribution for an anthology he
was preparing. Their negotiations led to a meeting and
a discussion of Symons's own poetry which left the impression that her personality was "aggressive" and the
effect of her conversation was "rather wearing." Symons
noted her condescension toward Graves as well as himself
and perceived a connection between her "insistence on
purity in poetic speech and an accompanying close finicki-
ness in personal relationships." Her tendency towards
"extreme individualism and poetic isolation" represented
"an aspect of literary life in the thirties that is now
too little recognised."

H110 Crane, Hart. *The Letters of Hart Crane, 1916-1932.* Ed.
Brom Weber. Berkeley and Los Angeles: University of
California Press, 1965.

Several letters refer to Riding. They offer a glimpse
of her at the beginning of her poetic career.

H111 Higginson, Fred H. *A Bibliography of the Works of
Robert Graves*. Hamden, Conn.: Archon Books, 1966.

Higginson cites works on which Riding and Graves collaborated, reviews of these books, and a letter by
Riding alone defending Graves's *Poems, 1929* from a
critical review (C14).

H112 Jensen, James. "The Construction of *Seven Types of
Ambiguity*." *Modern Language Quarterly*, 27 (September,
1966), 243-259.

Although his subject is Empson's book, Jensen becomes

involved in the controversy over who invented the "New
Criticism," a dispute which involves the Fugitive Group
in America and Robert Graves and Laura Riding in England.
In the first edition, Empson acknowledges a debt to
Graves's analysis of a Shakespeare sonnet in *A Survey of
Modernist Poetry*, but this book was written by Laura
Riding *and* Robert Graves. In a note appended to the
article, Graves claims he wrote the analysis of poems,
and Riding was responsible for the general principles.
Empson also adds a complicating comment: he says he
found the method of analysis in a book Graves had
written earlier--he simply named the wrong book. Riding
disputes Graves's claim in a letter the magazine published a few years later (C44). She also disputes
Louise Cowan's effort to credit the Fugitives with
originating the New Criticism.
    Jensen argues that Graves fused the methods of ana-
lyzing the subconscious which W.H.R. Rivers had taught
him with the heightened consciousness Riding demonstrated
to produce the "strenuous" textual analysis of *A Survey*.

H113   O'Connor, Frank (pseud. of Michael O'Donovan). *My
         Father's Son*. London: Macmillan, 1968.

    O'Connor's autobiography includes an account of
Geoffrey Phibbs, who was the immediate cause of Riding's
suicide attempt in 1929. O'Connor visited the houseboat
moored in the Thames that housed Nancy Nicholson and her
children with Phibbs, Graves, and Riding. Although he
avoids mentioning names, O'Connor makes his subject
clear by alluding to Riding's treatment of him as "Handy
Andy" in her novel *14A* (A21). His portrait of Phibbs
includes the epithet "Satanic," which becomes significant
when compared with Riding's habit of referring to him
as the Devil in her writing in the early 1930's. Phibbs
later changed his name to Taylor because his father
protested his adultery.

H114   Brown, Susan Jenkins. "Hart Crane: The End of Harvest."
         The Southern Review, 4 (Autumn, 1968), 945-1014. Rpt.
         in *Robber Rocks, Letters and Memories of Hart Crane,
         1923-1932*. Middletown, Conn.: Wesleyan University
         Press, 1969, pp. 36, 40.

    This memoir of Hart Crane includes several letters Crane
wrote as well as Brown's own recollections of Riding and
Crane. She reports that Crane called "the engrossing
female" he saw at many parties in New York "Rideshalk-
Godding" until he changed his name for her to "Laura
Riding Roughshod."

H115 Burns, Albert W. "Robert Graves and Laura Riding: A
      Literary Partnership." *DAI*, 30 (1969), 2014A–2015A
      (Diss. Boston U. 1969).

   Burns's title angered Riding when he told her of his
   plan, but they maintained a correspondence in which she
   tried to convey her view of her so-called "partnership"
   with Graves. She was not flattered by the suggestion
   that she influenced Graves; on the contrary, she regrets
   that she influenced him so little.

H116 Cunard, Nancy. *These Were the Hours, Memories of My
      Hours Press, Réanville and Paris, 1928-1931*. Ed. with
      a Foreword by Hugh Ford. Carbondale and Edwardsville:
      Southern Illinois University Press; London and
      Amsterdam: Feffer & Simons, 1969.

   In chapters on "Robert Graves: *Ten Poems More*, Laura
   Riding: *Twenty Poems Less*" and "Laura Riding: *Four Unposted Letters to Catherine*," Cunard recalls the circumstances in which these books were produced as well as
   the reception they received at the time. Her impression
   of Riding in 1929 was bifurcated: "Distinctly super-
   natural? Is that what she is? I asked myself. No,
   indistinctly, vaguely so. Her personality was very
   tense, dominating, and quietly American.... In this
   mystified state I could see two things clearly: her
   quality and her meticulousness." Riding and Graves
   suggested that Len Lye design the covers of their companion volumes, and Cunard offers an interpretation of
   the symbolism of his photomontages. He also designed
   the covers of *Four Unposted Letters to Catherine*, which
   Cunard, like other critics she mentions, preferred to
   Riding's more "difficult" work. Ford's foreword
   examines the proliferation of private presses between
   the wars, and he provides a bibliography of Hours Press
   publications.

H117 Kirkham, Michael. *The Poetry of Robert Graves*. London:
      Athlone Press, 1969.

   Examining the development of Graves's poetry, Kirkham
   describes Riding's influence on the themes and style of
   his work. Her desire to isolate "self" from "historic
   time" became the foundation of Graves's self-imposed
   exile and disregard of his readers. He celebrates her
   values in "Against Kind," "The Age of Certainty," most
   directly. The fourth, fifth, and sixth chapters focus
   on Graves's years with Riding when her moral and intellectual ethic formed the center of his myth. She guided

him from "unhappy withdrawal to militant rejection of
society, from involuntary to voluntary exile." Kirkham
shows the relationship between Riding's ideas and
Graves's conception of the "White Goddess." The con-
clusions about Riding in this book are based on Kirkham's reading of her *Collected Poems*, *Anarchism Is Not
Enough*, and *The World and Ourselves*; his subsequent
acquaintance with more of her work apparently altered
his views.

H118   Fuller, Roy. "The White Goddess." *the Review*, 23
       (1970), 3-9. (Cover of this issue reproduces photo-
       graph of Laura Riding in the 1930's. See frontis-
       piece.)

A summary of Laura Riding's career and the crucial
events in her life is the foundation of a critical
estimate of the woman many consider the incarnation of
Graves,'s conception of the "White Goddess." Admiring
especially "Lucrece and Nara" and Riding's use of the
four-beat line, Fuller attributes the defects of her
poetry to her "ideological obsession" that her poems
should "tell the truth." Her requirement surpassed
Owen's goal of making poetry truthful to *experience* and
aimed at a universal, eternal reality. Fuller seeks the
sources of Riding's failures: "But the intellect, as
has been seen, had to work with emotions of equal inten-
sity, and I think the final verdict must be that the
partnership was infrequently in balance. Her role as a
critic may be evidenced. Books like *Anarchism Is Not
Enough* and *Contemporaries and Snobs* are exasperatingly
unsatisfactory—so much brilliance, so much unwillingness
to keep on a sensible level of intelligibility; so much
insight, so much superior dogmatism." Riding replied
in C42.

H119   Seymour-Smith, Martin. "Laura Riding's 'Rejection of
       Poetry.'" *the Review*, 23 (1970), 10-14.

Although ignored by the majority, Laura Riding always
impressed a minority with her intelligence and poetic
skill. Nevertheless, readers have had to overcome difficulties posed by her "uncompromising, intractable and
intransigent attitude" and by the view of poetry as the
repository of truth which led to her rejection of poetry.
Her manner—"off-puttingly severe, obscure and hostile;
even paraphrenic"—seems at odds with her messianic
purpose first as a poet, then as a reconstituter of
words' meanings. She perceived a discrepancy between

poetry's ambition to utter truth and its vain, self-
loving, sensuous craft. Her abandonment of poetry is
most meaningful as a rejection of her own conception of
poetry: "More seriously, we must ask ourselves if this
rejection of poetry is not in fact a sublimation of its
author's rejection of certain of her own human circumstances; if the vices she attributes to poetry are not,
after all, those of human life itself; if the condition
of unconfusion for which she hopes is not as universally
accessible as she believes." Riding replied in C42.

H120   Saunders, John. "New Poetry." *Stand*, 11 (1970), 68-72.

Finding Riding's uncompromising attitude in her
prefaces and poems oppressive, Saunders identifies the
qualities of her poetry but finds them unlikable: "The
poems are at first compelling, then their hard brilliance
oppresses; one longs to escape from her 'Talking World';
although it is a world more exhausting than exhausted
and one will return to it."

H121   Tolley, A.T. "Rhetoric and the Moderns." *The Southern
Review*, 6 (Spring, 1970), 380-397.

Tolley takes Riding and Graves's *A Survey of Modernist
Poetry* as the antithesis to T.S. Eliot's school of
modernism. Riding and Graves represent the opposition
to the development of "individual style, ... rhetoric,
and traditional culture." They attempted to write "a
plain type of poetry whose form and diction were the
natural growth from an immediate and personal impulse."

H122   Hamilton, Ian. "Nothing But the Truth." *The Observer*,
9 August 1970, p. 20.

Reviewing Riding's *Selected Poems: In Five Sets*,
Hamilton identifies the premise from which her poetry
grew: "poetry should function, first and foremost, as a
tool of the abstractly questing intellect." Nevertheless, he finds her poems faulty both in intention and
execution: "As so often with profoundly cerebral authors
strong feeling seems to drive out, rather than enforce,
good sense: 'the reckless strum of hate,' 'the thistle
patch of memory,' 'the tattered throne of time'--poetry,
I think Miss Riding would agree, can get nearer to the
truth than this." Riding replied in C41.

H123   Fuller, Roy. [Letter.] *the Review*, 24 (December, 1970),
77.

Reply to letter from Laura (Riding) Jackson (C42) appearing in the same issue.

H124   Grigson, G. [Letter.] *the Review*, 24 (December, 1970), 78.

Reply to letter from Laura (Riding) Jackson (C42) appearing in the same issue.

H125   Kemp, Harry. [Letter.] *the Review*, 24 (December, 1970), 78.

Reply to letter from Laura (Riding) Jackson (C42) appearing in the same issue.

H126   Seymour-Smith, Martin. [Letter.] *the Review*, 24 (December, 1970), 77.

Reply to letter from Laura (Riding) Jackson (C42) appearing in the same issue.

H127   Cave, Roderick. *The Private Press*. New York: Watson-Guptill Publications, 1971.

Cave summarizes the development of Riding and Graves's Seizin Press and Nancy Cunard's Hours Press in a chapter titled, "England Between the Wars II: Backwaters and Tributaries," pp. 199-215, and quotes Riding's recollections of her original goals for the Press. Cave attributes the proliferation of small private presses in this period to the desire of modernist poets to circumvent the restraints commercial publishers imposed.

H128   Rosenthal, M.L. "Olson/His Poetry." *The Massachusetts Review*, 12 (Winter, 1971), 45-57.

Rosenthal examines Riding's effort to explore "the possibility of using words in poetry with the true voice and the true mind of oneself" to illuminate Charles Olson's work. Since Blake and the *Lyrical Ballads*, Rosenthal says, poets have tried to assimilate dissimilar modes of speech. In her 1962 BBC broadcast (G1), Riding said poetry was *in extremis*, and Rosenthal takes this characterization as a central insight into modern poetry.

H129   Kirkham, Michael. "Laura Riding's Poems." *The Cambridge Quarterly*, 5 (Spring, 1971), 302-308.

Reviewing *Selected Poems*, Kirkham summarizes Riding's aims as a poet as well as the moral reasons for her renunciation of poetry. He attributes the "difficulty"

of her poetry not to verbal obscurity but rather to the
originality and concentration of her ideas, particularly
her conceptions of truth, finality, and death. In a detailed analysis of the short poem "Afternoon," Kirkham
describes the characteristic "plot" of many other poems:
"first a cryptic statement of the thought, using the
basic elements of the poem's imagery--like a closed bud;
then a gradual unfolding of the thought's intricacies;
finally, in the last three lines, a rounding-back to the
original general statement, further reduced to its es-
sentials and set in a life-context of the widest coverage."
Seeking general truths, she mentions particular cases of
the central thought. The instances are conceived as
correspondences rather than as metaphors.

H130 ————. [Letter.] *the Review*, 26 (Summer, 1971), 55.

Reply to Harry Kemp's letter published earlier (H125).

H131 Ford, Hugh. "The Seizin Press." *The Private Library*,
n.s. 5 (Autumn, 1972), 121-138. Rpt. in *Published in
Paris: American and British Writers, Printers and
Publishers in Paris 1920-1939*. New York: Macmillan,
1975, pp. 385-403.

Ford's history is influenced by his correspondence
with Riding, who also appended a postscript to his
article (C48). He presents her view of the aims of the
Press: "An early vision of possibilities of going beyond
the merely literary in expressiveness entered into the
founding ideas of the Press. She describes her contribution to them as the conception that objectives in
writing should transcend the boundaries of 'literary
objectives as traditionally, and also modernistically,
understood,' and that standards of a 'goodness exceeding
literary notions of goodness' should be the critical
guide." Ford describes the content of each Seizin publication, reproduces several facsimile pages, and quotes
liberally from letters Riding wrote him concerning his
article.

H132 Clark, Alan. "The One Story: Laura (Riding) Jackson,
'The Telling,' and Before." *Stand*, 15 (1973), 32-37.
Portions reprinted in *Chelsea*, 33 (September, 1974),
160-161.

Privileged to be Riding's current amanuensis, Clark
presents a faithful picture of her current assessment
of her career, the importance of her renunciation of
poetry, and the purpose of *The Telling*.

H133 [Davie, Donald.] "An Ambition Beyond Poetry." *Times*
      Literary Supplement, 9 February 1973, p. 151. Rpt. in
      The Poet in the Imaginary Museum, Essays of Two
      Decades. Ed. Barry Alpert. Manchester: Carcanet,
      1977, pp. 249-254.

      Davie places Riding as the terminus of the line of
      poetic development originating from Keats's "Beauty is
      Truth, Truth Beauty." Her bravery and honesty made her
      face the falsity of this proposition and renounce poetry.
      But Davie points out that Riding forgets that Keats's
      assertion contradicted the warnings of Chaucer, Shake-
      speare, and Herbert, among others, that poetry was in
      fact far from truth. As fine as her poems are, he
      judges them to be too flawed to permit their author to
      disdain the craft of poetry. Turning from her poems to
      The Telling, Davie finds the tone of personal testimony
      more appealing than the self-righteousness of the Preface
      to her *Selected Poems*. Riding responded in C50.

H134 Kirkham, Michael. "Robert Graves's Debt to Laura
      Riding." *Focus on Robert Graves*, 3 (December, 1973),
      33-44.

      Kirkham's study of Robert Graves's poetry led him to
      an awareness of Riding's influence. To calculate the
      debt, he compares Graves's work with Riding's poems,
      essays, and stories that seem related thematically or
      verbally. He concludes that Riding is the major poet
      and Graves the minor one because her work attains a
      suprapersonal objectivity, while his is mired in personal
      emotion. Graves attempted to use her thought to supply
      his poetry with intellectual authority, but his inability
      to assimilate her ideas only added another element of
      conflict to his already turbulent work. Kirkham pre-
      sents examples which permit the reader to judge whether
      Graves is as indebted as Riding and Kirkham claim:
      "Laura Riding means what she says, is where the poem
      says she is; and this being so, we have participated in
      an experience that expands us: with Graves we have
      merely watched someone undergoing personal conflict,
      thrashing about, and coming to a token conclusion."

H135 McBride, Mary. [Review of *The Telling*.] *Library Journal*,
      1 December 1973, p. 3561.

      Reviewing *The Telling* briefly, McBride estimates its
      audience: "Devotees of Jackson will doubtless enjoy her
      probing exploration of the relation between the Self and

the Whole ..., but the general reader will find it a
rather disjointed admixture of the puzzling and the
obvious."

H136 Wexler, Joyce Piell. "Laura Riding: A Checklist."
      Four Decades of Poetry, 1 (January, 1974), 58-65.

      In deference to Riding's demands, this checklist is
      incomplete.

H137 [Review of *Selected Poems: In Five Sets*.] *Booklist*,
      15 April 1974, p. 901.

      Favorable review describes Riding's poems: "Poetry
      in the disciplined classical mode, with the strong
      cadences and undertones of sharpened sensibility."

H138 Auster, Paul. "Itinerary." *Chelsea*, 33 (September,
      1974), 169-170.

      In contrast to his review of *The Telling* and *Selected
      Poems* a year later (H146), Auster accepts Riding's re-
      nunciation of poetry: "Laura Riding is the first American
      poet to have accorded the poem the value and the dignity
      of a struggle. Turned in upon itself, challenging its
      very right to exist, the poem, in her hands, becomes
      act rather than object, transparence rather than thing....
      Everything takes place in absence, in the distance be-
      tween word and utterance, and each poem emerges at the
      moment there is nothing left to say." His later con-
      clusion is that her expectations of poetry and renuncia-
      tion resulted from her unique ideas; here he concludes
      that all of us must follow her: "And if she herself now
      looks upon her poetic work as having reached the end
      of poetic possibilities, it is in this end that we must
      look for a new beginning. And through her wall that we
      must pass."

H139 Davis, Robert Gorham. "Desperate for Truth." *Chelsea*,
      33 (September, 1974), 171.

      Defending himself from Riding's charge in *The Telling*
      that he accepts incertitude rather than pursue truth,
      Davis claims he longs for truth as much as she does:
      "The warranty for the truth of *The Telling* is a myth, a
      myth of literally remembering the Whole, the One, that
      preceded the existence of separate selves and that can,
      properly responded to, guide us toward unimaginable
      transcendence in the future. This gives Laura Riding
      assurance to speak on all manner of public subjects in

a way that is fascinating, frustrating, infuriating, il-
luminating. The private experience, however, that
created her certitude, that revealed the myth, remains
obscured, incomplete, expressed in a generalized language
that cannot bear the burdens imposed upon it."

H140   Katz, Joseph. "An Open Letter to *Chelsea*." *Chelsea*,
          33 (September, 1974), 164–165.

After weathering the difficulties of negotiating with
Riding about an article, Katz expresses this assessment:
"I think it must be painful to be Laura Riding Jackson.
From her letters and her books I believe that she is a
tough person ... strong and vulnerable at the same
time." She not only refuses to compromise with anything
less than complete knowledge, but also insists that we
refuse to compromise.

H141   Kirkham, Michael. "Laura (Riding) Jackson." *Chelsea*,
          33 (September, 1974), 140–150.

Kirkham compares the religious seriousness of Riding's
work, especially her "evangel" *The Telling*, to Paul
Tillich's idea of God as "the ground of being." Both
distinguish the false view that truth is an object, "out
there," from their beliefs that truth is the subjective
basis of our being. Afterwards, Kirkham tries to illuminate Riding's work by contrasting it with Graves's
distortions of her thought and imagery. This part of
the article is based on his "Robert Graves's Debt to
Laura Riding" (H134). Riding responded in C55.

H142   Mason, Ellsworth. "A Note." *Chelsea*, 33 (September,
          1974), 166.

As editor of *Focus on Robert Graves*, Mason is likely
to have received private instruction from Riding on the
proper way to read Riding. His note demonstrates what
he learned: "But in the long run, it is likely that
Laura Jackson will surpass Laura Riding (the two at
first compacted together, then gradually separating)
when, as is bound to happen, she is recognized as one
of the deepest, most subtle, most centrally aware
philosophical minds of this century."

H143   [Raiziss, Sonia.] "Plural Matters Singularly Told."
          Chelsea, 33 (September, 1974), 162–163.

As editor of *Chelsea*, Sonia Raiziss was responsible
for publishing Riding's current views on poetry as well

as *The Telling*. In a symposium of writers she invited
to comment on Riding's work, apparently with Riding's
approval, she offers an effusive account of her acquaintance with Riding's work: "What I want to say is: her
work in its many forms cannot be considered as random
literary spawn but deliberate issue of the same systematic
center of importance. Her world is a tough imaginative
planet, with its tensions of predetermined change where
the pressurized strata in the rock tell you all the hap-
penings of its history. Meanwhile, the components
suffer a feverish atomic spinning inside the steady
surface of matter. Matter instructed by its own intelligence of terrible endeavor."

H144 Sutherland, Donald. "To Gloss or Not." *Chelsea*, 33
(September, 1974), 167-169.

Apologizing for asking Riding to provide additional
glosses to her gospel, Sutherland questions her use of
certain words in *The Telling*. Especially troubling are
the meanings of "soul," "Being," and "One." In spite
of Riding's assurance that she avoided stylistic considerations, he finds her writing aesthetically seduc-
tive: "Also the rhetoric, the ordering of words through
sentences, is so handsomely and forcibly conducted that
one can enjoy it without attending to the meaning. An
esthetical reading has its dangers and perhaps there
should be warning signals against them, in notes or
glosses."

H145 Thurman, Judith. "Forgeries of Ourselves." *The Nation*,
30 November 1974, pp. 570-571.

Reviewing Riding's *Selected Poems*, Thurman praises the
poems that deal with Riding's attitudes to women: "She
has written some of the finest feminist poems I know:
'I Am'; 'The Divestment of Beauty'; and especially, 'The
Auspice of Jewels,' which is a classic by any standard...." Riding replied in C59.

H146 Auster, Paul. "The Return of Laura Riding." *New York
Review of Books*, 7 August 1975, pp. 36-38.

Auster perceives connections between Riding's poems
and *The Telling* that unify her superficially disjointed
career. Her desire to realize truth in language is
constant; only her method has changed. Her rejection
of poetry was implicit in her unique conception of what
poetry should be. Nevertheless, he considers her poems

the work that will be read and remembered. Riding replied in C60.

H147   Atlas, James. [Review of *Selected Poems*.] *Poetry*, 125
       (Fall, 1975), 295-297.

       Atlas attempts to ignore the "sheer nerve of her self-
       evaluations" in the Preface to appreciate that "a fine
       integrity can be seen in her attitude to poetry...."
       He finds the poems "highly compressed, intellectual,
       disciplined."

H148   Clark, Alan. "Robert Graves's Collected Poems." [Let-
       ter.] *Times Literary Supplement*, 23 January 1976,
       p. 85.

       Clark defends Riding against the characterization of
       the Seizin Press and Graves's use of the White Goddess
       myth in Ruth Padel's review of his *Collected Poems*, TLS,
       26 December 1975: "But the 'doctrine' only began to
       'emerge' after Laura Riding's presence was removed."
       Clark quotes Riding's letter (C36) deprecating the myth:
       "God of this, God of that, talk is rubbish in any
       period."

H149   Peterson, Richard F. "T.S. Eliot, Robert Graves and *The
       Criterion*." *ICarbS*, 3 (Summer-Fall, 1976), 69-73.

       Peterson reports on the contents of some of Graves's
       letters to Eliot that are part of the manuscript collec-
       tion held by Southern Illinois University at Carbondale.
       Graves proposed to Eliot that they collaborate on a book
       about modern poetry. Eliot declined because he was too
       busy, and Graves eventually found a partner in Laura
       Riding. Later, Graves wrote Eliot to protest John Gould
       Fletcher's review (H2) of Riding's *The Close Chaplet*.

**H150 Jacobs, Mark, and Alan Clark. "The Question of Bias:
       Some Treatments of Laura (Riding) Jackson." *Hiroshima
       Studies in English Language and Literature*, 21 (Summer,
       1976), 1-27.

H151   Canary, Robert H. "The Riding-Graves Seminar at the
       MLA." *Focus on Robert Graves*, 5 (June, 1976), 85-86.

       Canary reports on the papers presented at the seminar
       held in 1975 and Laura (Riding) Jackson's comments on
       them. Riding objected to "A View of Robert Graves"
       which concentrated on the respective roles of Riding and

Graves in *A Survey of Modernist Poetry*; she condemned
"Laura Riding's Pursuit of Truth" by Joyce Wexler and
protested the name of the seminar because it yoked her
name to Graves's.

H152   Matthews, T.S. *Jacks or Better, A Narrative*. New York:
         Harper and Row, 1977.

In his second effort at autobiography, Matthews fills
in all the silences in his earlier book. He focuses on
his days in Majorca with Riding and Graves and tries to
portray the extraordinary influence Riding had on all
their lives. His account is the frankest and most
analytical portrait of her available. Because he knew
Schuyler B. Jackson well, and in fact introduced him to
Riding, Matthews is also able to compare Riding's relationship with Graves to her second marriage. Of particular interest are Matthews' accounts of *No Decency
Left* (p. 145), his own novel *The Moon's No Fool* (p. 149),
the Protocol Riding and her circle wrote in 1939
(p. 156), and memories of the origin of *Epilogue*, including the explanation that she used the pseudonym
"Madeleine Vara" because she wrote so much of the review
herself (pp. 151, 319).

H153   Woolf, Virginia. *The Letters of Virginia Woolf*. Ed.
         Nigel Nicholson. Vol. 3. London: Hogarth Press,
         1977, pp. 226, 283n, 298.

Woolf, in a letter of 26 July 1926, refers to a "play
by a German Jewess," which the editor guesses is *The
Close Chaplet* by Laura Gottschalk but is probably
Voltaire, a long poem in dramatic form that Hogarth
also published.

H154   Atlas, James. "Riding Off." *London Magazine*, n.s. 16
         (February/March, 1977), 96-97.

Atlas responds to Riding's letter (C65).

H155   Norris, Christopher C. "Laura Riding's *The Telling*:
         Language, Poetry, and Neutral Style." *Language and
         Style*, 11 (Summer, 1978), 137-145.

In a serious evaluation of Riding's claims to being a
truth-teller, Norris compares her ideas to those of other
linguistic philosophers like Wittgenstein, W.M. Urban,
Kenneth Burke, Kathleen Nott, Coleridge, and William

Empson. Norris concludes, "*The Telling* is philosophical-
ly a case of idealism *expressed*, not of rationalism tried
or proven, through language." Contrary to her purpose,
which is to eschew the craft of poetry to serve her
creed, the argument rests on poetic methods: "Where the
pressure of telling becomes too great, as in Riding's
text, the balance [between creative and philosophic
discourse] is lost and the language restored more firmly
than ever to the realm of impure poetry and suasive
special pleading."

H156   Wexler, Joyce Piell. "Construing the Word: An Introduc-
       tion to the Writings of Laura (Riding) Jackson."
       DAI, 38 (July, 1977), 270-A (Diss. Northwestern 1974).

       Riding cooperated with this study and permitted a
       great deal of quotation from unpublished writings.
       When she read an early draft, she imposed restrictions
       on the subsequent use of these quotations.

H157   Woolf, Virginia. *The Letters of Virginia Woolf*. Ed.
       Nigel Nicholson. Vol. 4. London: Hogarth Press,
       1978, pp. 327-329.

       Woolf wrote Ethel Smyth that Riding's letters to
       editors hurt "The Cause" by demonstrating the "vanity
       of women": "Laura Riding ... I despise for writing per-
       petually to explain her own cause when reviewers say
       what is true--that she is a damned bad poet." Woolf's
       unkind remarks should be weighed against the fact that
       her Hogarth Press was nevertheless publishing Riding's
       poems.

H158   Wexler, Joyce Piell. *Laura Riding's Pursuit of Truth*.
       Athens: Ohio University Press, 1979.

       This full-length study brings pertinent biographical
       information to bear on a critical examination of all
       Laura Riding's work. This approach uncovers the meaning
       in her most obscure writing, the poems she wrote in the
       early 1930's after her suicide attempt, and demonstrates
       the constants underlying the superficial changes in her
       career. Valuing the poems most, Wexler finds the
       source of their quality in Riding's beliefs: "The moral
       rigor and aesthetic fervor motivating the poet produced
       a verbal integrity that demonstrated her belief that
       every word should be not only effective but also true.
       Trying to wrench both cosmic and aural harmonies from
       language, Riding made her poems vibrate with the inten-

sity of her effort to pursue thought to its source."
Her poems "portray a mind locked in combat with words
and winning."

When Riding applied her convictions to her personal
life, the results were less successful. Wexler notes:
"Refusing to be flexible, to tolerate dissent, or to
value variety, Riding provoked disorder in the singleness
of her quest for perfect order. She was not satisfied
to look for what is constant in life; her aim was also
to convert the essentially dynamic aspects of life into
constants. When she applied her standards of perfection
to her friends, it was they who were found to be im-
perfect."

H159 ————. "Laura Riding's Pursuit of Truth." *The Barat
Review*, 7 (Spring, 1979), 12-16.

This account of Riding's work incorporates Wexler's
personal impressions after spending a few days in Wabasso,
Florida, where Riding lives. Wexler assesses Riding's
claim that her work demonstrates a single purpose, truth-
telling, by briefly examining her career. A detailed
analysis of the poem "Death as Death" leads to a survey
of Riding's themes related to significant biographical
information. The concluding paragraph reads: "Laura
Riding's career justifies her claim that a single moral
purpose has always motivated her, but her work also
reveals personal reasons that the search for what is
universal and unchanging in human experience has been
at the center of her life. Since the pursuit of truth,
as she conceived it, ministered to her deepest spiritual
needs, it became a sacrosanct creed. She willingly ex-
plained it to others, but she could not alter any part
of it without yielding her authority and control. Her
inner need for certainty determined both her conception
of truth and the tenacity with which she has upheld it."

H160 Symons, Julian. "Out of Time and Into Poetry." *Times
Literary Supplement*, 18 July 1980, pp. 795-796.

In a long review-essay on H158, Symons summarizes
Riding's career as it is presented in *Laura Riding's
Pursuit of Truth* and adds some details about the background of Geoffrey Phibbs, who figured in Riding's suicide
attempt. Symons, who admires and respects Riding's work,
offers his own assessment of her successes and failures,
concluding, "The final impression must be of original
genius spoiled, yet the best of them [the poems] are
extraordinary works, unlike anything else written in this
century. She was a mistress of the craft she deprecates."

H161   Clark, Alan. "Laura Riding." *Times Literary Supplement*,
       1 August 1980, p. 874.

       In a letter to the editor, Clark objects to H160 for
       failing to value Riding's non-poetic writing.

H162   Woolmer, J. Howard. "Geoffrey Phibbs." *Times Literary
       Supplement*, 8 August 1980, p. 896.

       In a letter to the editor, Woolmer supplements Symons's
       account of Geoffrey Phibbs in H160. Not only did Phibbs,
       using the pseudonym R. Fitzurse, publish the volume of
       poems *It Was Not Jones* in the "Hogarth Living Poets"
       series, but he also published and immediately withdrew
       a volume called *Withering of the Fig Leaf* (Hogarth
       Press, 1927).

H163   Nowell-Smith, Simon. "Geoffrey Phibbs." *Times Literary
       Supplement*, 22 August 1980, p. 936.

       In a letter to the editor, Nowell-Smith provides an
       explanation for the publication and immediate withdrawal
       of Phibbs's *Withering of the Fig Leaf* as reported in
       H162. After several copies were sent out for review,
       Phibbs heeded warnings from his friends that the anti-
       Catholic content of the poems would cost him his job as
       a Carnegie librarian.

H164   [Review of *Laura Riding's Pursuit of Truth*.] *AB Book-
       man's Weekly*, 8 September 1980, p. 1340.

       Brief summary of H158 occasioned Riding's retort (C71).

H165   Symons, Julian. "Laura Riding." *Times Literary Sup-
       plement*, 19 September 1980, p. 1039.

       In a letter to the editor, Symons responds to Riding's
       objections (C70) to his review of H158.

INDEX OF POEMS

INDEX OF STORIES

GENERAL INDEX

(references to roman numerals and to arabic
numbers without letter prefixes are to pages;
all other references are to item numbers)